RELISH
MIDLANDS
The Heart Of England

Original recipes from the region's finest chefs

First Published 2012
By Relish Publications
Shield Green Farm, Tritlington,
Northumberland, NE61 3DX.

ISBN: 978-0-9564205-8-9

Publisher: Duncan L Peters
General Manager: Teresa Peters
Design: Vicki Brown
Relish Photography: Tim Green
Editorial Consultant: Paul Robertson
Senior Account Manager: Paul Bamber
Proof Assistant: Jack Bamber
Additional Content: James Day
www.leisuremarketingltd.co.uk
Additional Photography: Andy Richardson

Printed By: Balto Print Ltd, Stratford,
London E15 2TF.

RELISH
PUBLICATIONS.CO.UK

004
CONTENTS

006
CONTENTS

DESSERTS

Iced Mango Parfait, Pineapple Poached In Star Anise, Passion Fruit Sorbet, Coconut Rice, Mango Purée

Honey & Orange Cake, Chocolate, Blood Orange Honeycomb & Ice Cream

Dark Chocolate & Banana Fondant, Banana Milkshake, Caramelised Banana & Chocolate Ice Cream

Kaffir Lime Leaf Panna Cotta With Mango Soup, Macerated Mango & Black Pepper Shortbread

Dark Chocolate Caramel Cream, Jaffa Orange & Warm Vanilla Doughnuts

Refreshing Lemon Posset With Raspberry Sauce, Summer Berries & Shortbread Biscuits

Chai Panna Cotta, Mango Compote & Coconut Sorbet

Beetroot Frangipane With A Poppy Seed & Ginger Ice Cream

Pineapple & Pink Peppercorn Tarte Tatin

Vanilla Creme Brûlée, Strawberry, Honeycomb, Basil, White Balsamic Foam

Warwick Chocolate Brownie Truffles & Chocolate Sauce

Lemon Tart With Chantille Cream & Fresh Raspberries

RESTAURANTS

INTRODUCTION WITH ANDREAS ANTONA

In some ways, writing the foreword to this celebration of Midlands gastronomy is rather like being the Godfather. I am immensely proud, of course, to have been invited to write the opening section to a book that celebrates the best of our region's food.

I have long championed our unique cuisine: The Midlands was once a culinary desert, often the laughing stock of those 'in the know' but, in recent years the entire region has raised its game and blossomed into a region with worldwide acclaim. From the Michelin seeds that were planted over ten years ago in Kenilworth and Ludlow, to the young talent of chefs Adam Bennett and Kristian Curtis, who achieved a place representing the UK in the world food competition that is the renowned Bocuse D'or 2013.

Make no mistake, the Midlands is at the cutting edge of sensational cuisine.

So, with so much going for us, how can I describe myself as the Godfather? The answer is really straight forward. I feel a responsibility to the many great chefs and exceptional producers whose food is featured on these pages. They are devoted to excellent food and building an international reputation that will last for many years. I want those chefs and producers to succeed, to reach their potential and make sure that when the international audience thinks of great food, they think of the Midlands as readily as Paris or London.

I've enjoyed a long career and am proud to have held a Michelin star for some considerable time. But beyond my own achievements, one of my greatest pleasures has been to see exciting new cooks go on to become fine chefs in their own right.

My skills have been passed on to a new generation and it is truly exciting to see the way in which they are developing. The seeds for the future have already been sown and Midlands gastronomy is in capable hands.

Great eating is about clean, simple flavours, which rely on the finest ingredients. In many ways, the larder section for this book is as important as sections on the individual chefs. Without our great producers, we would flounder. The men and women who stock our shelves deserve enormous respect.

Relish is not just a celebration of Midlands food, however. It has a deeper meaning. Just as the region has spawned a new generation of world chefs, so I hope this book will inspire you, dear reader, to cook in the safety of your own kitchen.

The chefs featured here are nothing if not diverse. There are those who are avante garde and experimental, those who are staunchly traditional, those who favour innovative techniques and those whose big, robust flavours showcase the best of local ingredients.

And when you leaf through the pages of this book, I want you to have the confidence to experiment at home - not to be afraid of making mistakes. Cooking is one of life's greatest pleasures. I hope this showcase of Midlands talent gives you the inspiration to create exceptional cuisine and visit some of the fine venues across the region that is the Midlands.

Chef Andreas Antona
Simpsons Restaurant

010
AALTO
RESTAURANT
AT HOTEL LA TOUR

Albert Street, Birmingham, B5 5JT

0121 718 8000
www.hotel-latour.co.uk

A alto Restaurant at Hotel La Tour serves modern classics inspired by Marcus Wareing.

Head Chef Alex Penhaligon has worked alongside Michelin-starred Marcus and his team, to create a menu of flavoursome classic dishes.

Alex said: "Our emphasis is on creating a range of great dishes with a modern twist, produced freshly on site."

The result is presented at Aalto. Diners arrive at the restaurant from the striking entrance lobby of Hotel La Tour and through the Alvar Bar, which is fast becoming one of the city centre's places in which to see and be seen.

The hotel, which has 174 bedrooms and suites, opened in March 2012 and Alex and his team quickly set about establishing the restaurant on the city scene.

Using local artisan producers where possible, the aim is to showcase the best the region has to offer, with the menu at Aalto changing to reflect this. The restaurant's open kitchen format affords diners a great view of the team at work as they conjure up culinary magic.
The semi-circular, high level Kitchen Table, with sleek granite top, seats eight on stools and has a direct view of the kitchen. Private dining is available for parties of up to 16.

Aalto Restaurant at Hotel La Tour Birmingham presents
modern classics inspired by Marcus Wareing. The menu
changes regularly to present the best seasonal flavours,
making great use of the region's best artisan producers.

HARROGATE LOAF

SERVES 10

*St Cosme Little James Basket Press Viognier -
Sauvignon VDP D'OC 2010 (France)*

Ingredients

600g veal mince
500g unsmoked bacon
250g pork fat (finely diced)
125g chicken livers (diced)
175ml port
175ml Madeira
175ml brandy
1 large onion (thinly sliced)
1 clove of garlic (finely chopped)
1 dstp thyme leaves (picked)
25g green peeled pistachios
streaky bacon slices (to line a large loaf tin)
salt and pepper (to season)
handful of flat leaved parsley (chopped)
a few capers in brine
vinaigrette dressing
1 tbsp vegetable oil

Method

Gently cook the onions and garlic in the vegetable oil. In a separate pan, reduce the alcohol to a syrup. Add the veal mince, unsmoked bacon, pork fat and chicken livers to the onion mix and stir in the reduced alcohol. Add the thyme leaves and pistachios and season with salt and pepper.

Line a large loaf tin with clingfilm and streaky bacon. Spoon the mixture into the tin and press down firmly. Cover with foil and cook at 180°C for one and a half hours. Remove from the oven, place a weight on top of the loaf to compress and leave to cool.

To Serve

Mix the parsley with the capers and vinaigrette. Turn out the terrine, slice and serve with the dressing.

Chef's Tip
Wrapped well in clingfilm and foil, Harrogate Loaf freezes well.

CORNISH SEA BASS, CREAMED LEEK, MUSSELS, GRAIN MUSTARD

SERVES 4

🍷 *Mad Fish Riesling*
(Australia)

Ingredients

Sea Bass

4 large Cornish sea bass fillets
(scaled, pin boned and with skin scored)
1 large leek (white only, shredded)
500g mussels (de-bearded and steamed
in a pan with a large glass of white wine
and a splash of water)
1 dstp of grain mustard
250ml double cream
a little vegetable oil or sunflower oil (to cook)
knob of butter
salt and pepper (to season)

Mussel Cream Sauce

200ml liquor from the cooked mussels
250ml chicken stock
250ml double cream
salt and pepper (to season)
roux made with equal amounts of unsalted
butter and plain flour

Method

For The Sea Bass

Pour the cream into a saucepan and heat until thick then add the grain mustard. Fry the leeks in butter until soft and add a spoonful of the cream mixture. Add the mussels and heat through.

Season the sea bass with salt and pepper, heat the oil in a shallow pan and fry the fish, skin side down, until crisp and golden. Continue to cook for approximately two to three minutes, depending on the size of the fillets, until the fish is cooked through.

> **Chef's Tip**
>
> To ensure the skin on the sea bass crisps well, ensure the pan is nice and hot.

For The Mussel Cream Sauce

Reduce the chicken stock and mussel *liquor* to half volume. Add the double cream, bring to a boil and reduce a little - not too much or the sauce will be too salty. Whisk in the *roux* a spoonful at a time until the sauce begins to thicken, reduce the heat and simmer for approximately ten minutes.

Pass through a sieve.

To Serve

Place the leek, mussel and cream mixture in the centre of individual serving dishes.

Place the sea bass on top. Serve the mussel cream sauce in a separate jug or pour over the fish.

JAFFA CAKE PUDDING

SERVES 4

 *Rivesaltes Ambre NV
(France)*

Ingredients

Sponge

125g softened butter
zest of 2 oranges
225g caster sugar
3 large free range eggs
110g plain flour
10g baking powder
60g sour cream

Candied Orange

1 large orange
100g orange marmalade
100g caster sugar

Chocolate Ganache Sauce

50g 80% dark chocolate
100g double cream
1 tbsp Cointreau

Method

For The Candied Orange

Cut the orange into 2mm thick slices and place in a pan.
Add the marmalade and sugar and bring to the boil.
Simmer over a low heat until the slices are translucent.
Strain and reserve the juice.

For The Sponge

Beat the butter, orange zest and sugar until creamy and thick.
In a separate bowl, beat the eggs and sour cream and add
into the butter and orange zest mixture, mix until smooth and
well blended.

Mix together the flour and baking powder and fold into the egg
mixture. Place into individual muffin cases or buttered moulds,
lined with candied oranges and bake at 160°C for 20 minutes.

When cooled, gently ease the sponges out of the cases or
moulds, pour marmalade syrup into the bottom of each, and
replace the cakes. Leave to cool.

For The Chocolate Ganache

Add the Cointreau to the double cream and heat until steaming.
Pour over the chocolate and stir well until melted and smooth.

> **Chef's Tip**
> For extra depth of flavour use Valrhona chocolate

To Serve

Ease the sponges with the candied orange out of the mould and
pour over the chocolate ganache. Serve with cream or ice cream.

CASTLE HOUSE

Castle Street, Hereford, Herefordshire, HR1 2NW

01432 356 321
www.castlehse.co.uk

Head Chef - Claire Nicholls
Wine Selection - Mike Lowe

Tucked away in an elegant quarter of Hereford, a two minute walk from the magnificent Cathedral, Castle House is a boutique townhouse hotel owned by a Herefordshire farming family.

With its elegant Grade II listed Georgian architecture, 24 luxurious suites or bedrooms, and terraced garden leading down to the old Hereford castle moat, Castle House has a very relaxed and informal atmosphere. The Restaurant and Castle Bistro, among the finest in Herefordshire, are the domain of Claire Nicholls, who sources her ingredients from local farmers and producers, as well as the owner's nearby Ballingham Farm.

Claire has worked at Castle House for more than 11 years and as Head Chef for nearly eight. Passionate about food from an early age, she started cooking at the age of six! Claire trained at Hereford Technical College and the acclaimed Birmingham College of Food. While living in Hong Kong for two years, she discovered a love for Asian food which has influenced her cooking, but Claire is steeped in her roots, sourcing produce from the Marches and, when possible, pedigree Hereford beef and lamb reared by George Watkins on the family's farm.

Claire admits "I am so lucky because Herefordshire has an abundance of fruit and vegetable producers, most of whom I know personally. We are most famous for our apple and pear orchards but there is so much more! Great asparagus, wild game, pedigree Hereford beef, rare breed pork and lamb. Our strawberries, raspberries and blackcurrants rival most other UK counties' soft fruits and local Farmhouse cheeses are outstanding. We may be a small county (sometimes confused with one north of London) but we've got a lot to talk about and be proud of."

Photograph by Simon Milton

Since buying the hotel in 2006, owner David Watkins continues to invest in Castle House's future, ensuring it maintains its reputation for luxury and quality service. In 2008 he introduced the Castle Bar and Bistro, shortly followed by a new garden suite, the refurbishment of the rosetted restaurant and the opening of Number 25, a Georgian townhouse with eight luxury guestrooms, just yards from the hotel. Most recently the very popular garden terrace has been extended for more *al fresco* diners.

Castle House is the perfect base for breaks in Hereford and the Wye Valley. From here you can explore the charming city of Hereford with its world-famous Mappa Mundi and the breathtakingly beautiful countryside beyond.

With such an abundance of fresh, local produce at her fingertips, including the family's Ballingham farm, Claire Nicholls' Castle House menus reflect all that is great about Herefordshire. The award-winning restaurant is elegant not stuffy and the Castle Bar and Bistro is more informal. Afternoon tea is another favourite with locals and guests alike and the 'secret' terraced garden beside the old Hereford Castle moat is an absolute oasis in sunny weather.

GUINEA FOWL TERRINE, RIESLING JELLY, CARROTS & CUCUMBER

SERVES 6

*Churton Sauvignon Blanc, Marlborough 09
(New Zealand)
The wine has the pungency of a good
Marlborough Sauvignon Blanc, expressed by a
lovely minerality on the nose and palate.*

Ingredients

Terrine

6 Guinea Fowl legs
1 litre chicken stock
1 leaf of gelatine
5g parsley
5g chervil
salt and pepper

Jelly

100ml Riesling wine
1 leaf gelatine

Carrots And Cucumber

2 carrots
1/2 cucumber
100ml fresh orange juice
pinch of salt

Method

For The Terrine

Place the Guinea Fowl legs into a casserole dish, and then cover with the chicken stock. Place in an oven at 160°C for approximately one hour or until tender and falling off the bone.

Remove from the stock and flake the meat lightly into a bowl. Reserve 100ml of the *liquor*. Place one leaf of gelatine into cold water to soften, when soft place into the cooking *liquor* and dissolve. Chop the herbs and gently mix into the leg meat with salt and pepper to taste.

Line a small terrine mould or *dariole* with clingfilm. Put 2cm of the leg mix into the bottom of the terrine, then spoon about a tablespoon of the stock and gelatine mix onto it, and then repeat until the leg mix is used up. Fold over the edges of clingfilm to cover the terrine then weight it down and leave in the fridge to set for at least two hours.

For The Jelly

Warm 50ml of the Riesling in a saucepan and soften the gelatine in cold water. When soft add to the wine and dissolve. Remove from the heat and add the remaining 50ml of wine.

Pour into a small container approximately 5cm by 5cm lined with clingfilm and leave in the fridge to set for about two hours.

For The Garnish

Grate one of the carrots and cook with the orange juice for 15 minutes with a pinch of salt. Then blend till smooth. Peel the other carrot and cucumber to create strips for garnishing later.

To Serve

Turn out the terrine and slice, gently turn out the Riesling jelly and dice. Garnish with carrots.

RELISH MIDLANDS **CASTLE HOUSE**

(see glossary)
Photographs by Jay Watson

FILLET OF HEREFORD BEEF, ASPARAGUS, BRAISED SHIN, WATERCRESS SPAETZLE, CEPS

SERVES 4

Esterhazy Pinot Noir, 2010
(Austria)
Bit of a revelation to those new to Austrian wine,
this is a delicious forward mouthful, with all the
fruit of pinot noir but none of the farmyard.

Ingredients

4 x 170g fillet of beef
16 fresh asparagus spears
350g braised shin of beef
100g peas
300ml beef *jus*
4 ceps

Spaetzle

50g watercress
2 eggs
100g flour
salt and pepper

Method

For The Beef

Braise the beef shin well in advance, for about three hours in a low oven. Flake the meat and leave to one side. Trim the fillets and tie up into the size you like. Leave in the fridge until required.

For The Spaetzle

Place the watercress into a blender, leaving a few leaves for garnishing, and blend with the eggs and flour to form a smooth thick batter. Place a saucepan of water on to simmer, then pour the batter into a colander and push through into the water to make small dumplings. Poach for five minutes and place into iced water. Then drain.

For The Asparagus

Prepare the asparagus and *blanch* in boiling salted water for two minutes then plunge into iced water and drain.

For The Jus

Reduce the *jus* until it becomes sticky then fold in the shin meat.

Panfry the fillet for four minutes. Add the ceps, turn the fillet over and cook for a further four minutes. Now leave to rest for three minutes.

Warm the spaetzle in a little butter. Reheat the asparagus then add the peas to the shin mix.

To Serve

Cut the fillet through the centre, place two piles of spaetzle on a heated plate, and place the fillet halves on top. Make three piles of shin and scatter with asparagus and ceps.

(see glossary)
Photographs by Jay Watson

WHITE CHOCOLATE & WASABI ICED PAVE, STRAWBERRY LOLLY, STRAWBERRY SOUP

SERVES 4

Margan Botrytis Semillon Hunter Valley, 2008 (Australia)
Strikingly powerful fruit containing ripe aromas of lemon, fig and honey with great acidity and freshness.

Ingredients

Iced Pavé

14 egg yolks
250ml cream (semi-whipped)
70g sugar
40g white chocolate
1 tsp wasabi paste

Strawberry Lolly

125ml strawberry purée (90g strawberries blended with 35ml water)
50g sugar
2 gelatine leaves
squeeze of lemon juice
4 lolly sticks
4 egg cups

Strawberry Soup

100ml strawberry purée (100g blended strawberries)
50ml apple juice
10g sugar

Method

For The Iced Pavé

Place the egg yolks into a mixing machine and whisk until light and fluffy. Gently melt the chocolate in a bowl over a pan of simmering water (*bain-marie*.) Place the sugar into a saucepan with just enough water to dissolve it. Heat to 120°C, carefully pour onto the yolks whilst whisking and whisk until cool. Fold in the chocolate, wasabi and cream, place into 60mm rings and freeze for about three hours

For The Strawberry Lolly

Warm 50ml of the strawberry purée with the sugar and lemon juice, soak the gelatine in cold water until soft, remove and dissolve in the strawberry and sugar mix.

Add the rest of the purée and set over iced water. When nearly set, remove from ice, pour into the egg cups up to half way, place a lolly stick in the centre of each then set in fridge for ten minutes. Top up with the rest of the mix and return to the fridge until later.

For The Soup

Blend the strawberry purée with the apple juice and sugar to make the soup.

To Serve

Turn out the jellies gently by using the heat from your hands; use this method also for the pavés. Sprinkle a little icing sugar on a plate, sit the pavé on top, lie the jelly down then pour the soup into a shot glass and serve immediately!

(see glossary)

Photographs by Jay Watson

030
FAIRLAWNS

178 Little Aston Road, Aldridge, North Birmingham, WS9 0NU

01922 455 122
www.fairlawns.co.uk

The kitchens at the Fairlawns have been central in developing it from a modest eight bedroom guesthouse into a successful 60 bedroom hotel with spa. Set in a central location and surrounded by nine acres of landscaped grounds, the Fairlawns is ideal for exploring the West Midlands and is well connected to a number of key roads throughout the area.

The Pette family have owned and run the property for 28 years and central to its core values are a passion for food, wine, hospitality and service.

Head Chef Neil Atkins and his award-winning brigade cook English food that is influenced by flavours from around the world. Neil makes use of the Birmingham market to source most of the food that makes up its seasonal 'Market Menu'. He takes great pride in sourcing ingredients from the Midlands where possible along with using home gown herbs, rhubarb and apples.

Fairlawns also offers a 'Classic British Menu' which has developed a real following for customers wishing to sample good food that is cooked well, such as lobster thermidor, Dover sole or 21-day dry-aged beef.

The food is complemented by a mix of classic and modern wines chosen by John Pette Senior. John buys wines that he likes, along with award winning wines from around the world. He tends to buy these in small quantities and replaces them to suit tastes and with the next crop of award winners.

The Fairlawns aim to deliver consistently good quality food and good value for money. Central to doing so are the efforts of the friendly, efficient and helpful front of house staff who, supported by the kitchen, create an atmosphere in which customers can mark any occasion in style.

CITRUS MARINADE SALMON GRAVADLAX, ELEMENTS OF TARTAR, LEMON DRESSING

SERVES 8

🍷 *Bin 26, Domaine Wachau, Gruner Veltliner, 2008 (Austria)*
This is one of our award-winners, Gold and Trophy winner, Best Austrian Wine for Decanter World Wine Awards. Perfectly matched to this dish with fresh, fruity and peppery flavours. Also an ideal wine for an aperitif.

Ingredients

Salmon Gravadlax

1 side salmon (fillet and pin bone)
125g sea salt
150g caster sugar
2 oranges (juice and zest)
4 lemons (juice and zest)
2 limes (juice and zest)
100ml vodka

Lemon Dressing

2 lemons
30ml white wine vinegar
100ml rapeseed oil
20g caster sugar
1 egg yolk

Garnish

10g baby capers
10g gherkins (fine dice)
1 shallot (peeled and cut to small rings)
micro cress

Method

For The Salmon Gravadlax

Mix salt and sugar with citrus zest and rub into the salmon flesh. Mix vodka and citrus juice. Compress the salmon in a vacuum pack bag with juice and vodka for 36 hours.

For The Lemon Dressing

Mix sugar with egg yolk to a *sabayon*, add lemon and vinegar. Pour in the rapeseed oil slowly until it emulsifies.

To Serve

Thinly cut the salmon. Arrange alongside the shallot, gherkin and caper on a slate. Drizzle the lemon dressing over to serve.

LOCAL OUTDOOR REARED PORK THREE WAYS

SERVES 4

Bin 73, Bodegas Borsao Seleccion Barrica, 2008
(Spain)
*Old vines grown high in the mountains produce
a bright and juicy wine whose plum and vanilla
flavours are ideally suited to this celebration
of pork.*

Ingredients

1 pork fillet
1 local cured ham (sliced)
100g black pudding
1 pork belly
1/4 Savoy cabbage
1 Bramley apple
100ml brandy
2 Maris Piper potatoes
50ml double cream

Sauce

500ml veal stock
1 clove garlic
1 shallot
100ml red wine

Method

Wrap pork fillet in ham and wrap in clingfilm to hold the shape.

Slice black pudding into two discs.

Confit pork belly for 12 hours at 68°C, press overnight then cut in to 6cm x 2cm portions.

Finely shred cabbage and sweat down until tender.

Peel and chop apple, add brandy, cover and cook until soft, purée until smooth, place in a bottle for plating.

Gently heat cream and infuse with peeled and crushed garlic.

Peel and thinly slice the potato, layer up with the garlic cream then cook until tender at 160°C for approximately 35 to 40 minutes then cut out.

To make the sauce, cook the shallot and garlic until soft, without colour, add wine and reduce liquid by half, add the stock and reduce until you have the correct consistency.

To Serve

Squeeze apple purée out along the plate and arrange the cabbage. Take two slices of pork fillet and arrange with the black pudding. Brown the pork belly until crisp and arrange on the plate. Finish with the potato and sauce.

ARCTIC ROLL, TEXTURES OF BLACKBERRY

SERVES 8

🍷 *Bin 234, Campbells Rutherglen Muscat
(Australia)
Produced with the Muscat a petit grains rouge
grape, fresh raisin aromas, rich fruit, clean spirit
and a great length of flavour on the palate.*

Ingredients

Sponge

125g caster sugar
125g plain flour
4 eggs

Semifreddo Ice Cream Base

1 vanilla pod (seeds)
200ml whipping cream (semi-whip to soft peaks)
100ml water
150g caster sugar
5 egg yolks

Blackberry Crisp

300ml blackberry coulis (this can be made
beforehand by heating the fruit with sugar and
water. Purée then strain through a sieve)
60g *isomalt*

Blackberry Jelly

680g blackberry coulis
1kg caster sugar
57g pectin
57g caster sugar

Method

For The Sponge

Line a baking sheet with silicone paper. Whisk eggs and caster
sugar until they form a *sabayon*, then fold in sifted flour.
Cook at 180°C for ten minutes.

For The Semifreddo Ice Cream Base

Whisk the egg yolks then mix with water and sugar.
Keep whisking the *sabayon* until it reaches 120°C then put in
the mixer and whisk until cool.

Fold in semi-whipped cream with the vanilla seeds added.

Set in cylinder mounds in freezer.

For The Blackberry Crisp

Mix ingredients and boil to 120°C.

Spread out on *silpat* sheet and leave to dry for 24 hours at
90°C. After this time, cut with a sharp craft knife into strips of
1cm x 5cm.

For The Blackberry Jelly

Rub the pectin and 57g of caster sugar together. Boil the fruit
coulis and the 1kg of caster sugar together, add the pectin and
sugar to this and cook to 150°C. Pour into a tray to set, cut into
square dice for presentation.

To Serve

Spread a little blackberry jam onto sponge and wrap round
ice cream cylinders. Shape and cut into two pieces.
Assemble with all other components as in the picture.

040
THE FEATHERS HOTEL

The Bull Ring, Ludlow, Shropshire, SY8 1AA

01584 875 261
www.feathersatludlow.co.uk

The Feathers Hotel is one of the best known hotels in the United Kingdom. Its reputation is worldwide.

In 1983 the historian and author Jan Morris wrote in The New York Times:

"I dare say it is the most handsome inn in the world... everybody knows of it. It is one of the prime images of olde England, portrayed in posters and brochures wherever tourism is known."

The history of the hotel has been traced to the early 16th Century when it belonged to Thomas Hackluyt. In the early 17th Century it came into the hands of Rees Jones, a younger son of a gentry farmer from Pembrokeshire. He commissioned the rebuilding of the house in 1619.

Although the Feathers is renowned for its Jacobean façade, its origins are even more ancient, standing as it does in Ludlow's medieval town wall near the old Corve Gate.

This was one of seven gates that used to protect Ludlow. The town, which has been described as one of the most beautiful and historic in all England, was of strategic importance for centuries and was the administrative centre for Wales and the border counties.

Now its position has gained renewed importance for those who wish to enjoy the tranquil beauty of this unspoilt part of England.

The Feathers Hotel's head chef, Stuart Forman, left college with a Level 3 Management Course in Catering when he went to work at Bovey Castle in Devon for two and a half years, working under David Berry.

For seven years Stuart worked at the Selsdon Park Hotel under Alan White and Matt Ashton. Moving up the ranks, Stuart left in 2007 to work at the Feathers Hotel when he became head chef in 2010.

The food Stuart produces is modern British cuisine and wherever possible local produce and suppliers are used. The menus are changed seasonally to reflect this.

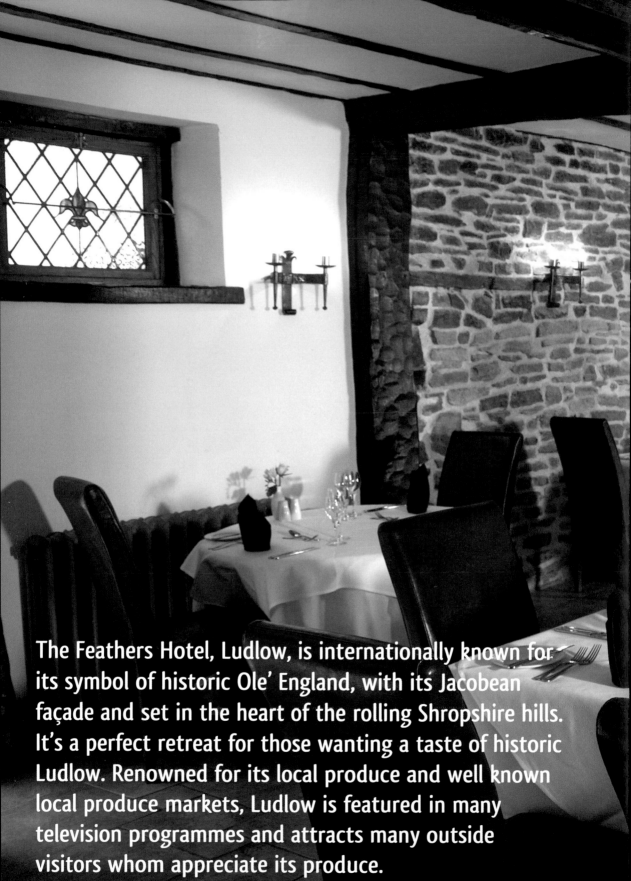

The Feathers Hotel, Ludlow, is internationally known for its symbol of historic Ole' England, with its Jacobean façade and set in the heart of the rolling Shropshire hills. It's a perfect retreat for those wanting a taste of historic Ludlow. Renowned for its local produce and well known local produce markets, Ludlow is featured in many television programmes and attracts many outside visitors whom appreciate its produce.

HONEY ROAST DUCK, SESAME CRUST, GINGER, SOY & HONEY DRESSING

SERVES 4

Wide River Shiraz
(South Africa)

Ingredients

2 duck breasts
1 orange (segmented)
3 spring onions (sliced)
1 medium beetroot
20g honey
4 gelatine leaves
1g red amaranth micro herbs
1g celery leaf
50ml hot water
10g sugar

Mousse

2 duck legs
175ml double cream
10g sesame seeds
5g chives (chopped)
salt and pepper
300g root vegetables
duck fat (to cover duck)

Dressing

10g ginger (finely chopped)
10ml soy sauce
10g honey
75ml olive oil
50ml white wine vinegar

Method

For The Duck

Seal off two duck breasts in a hot pan with no oil. Once the skin is well coloured, turn over and spread honey over the skin. Cook at 180°C for ten minutes.

For The Beetroot Jelly

Cook beetroot in boiling water for approximately 30 minutes or until tender with the skin on. Take out of water, peel off the skin and blitz into a purée adding fresh hot water to the right consistency. Add sugar and soaked gelatine and strain through sieve into a tray to set.

For The Mousse

Seal off legs in hot pan then sweat off root vegetables in the remaining oil. Add the duck on top of the vegetables and add duck fat to cover. Cover with foil and cook at 130°C for one hour 45 minutes until tender.

Drain off the fat and shred the meat.

Heat the cream to boiling point then blitz with the duck until smooth and soft. Leave to cool for ten minutes then add the chives and season.

Roll in a double layer of clingfilm in a cylinder shape and chill until set.

> **Chef's Tip**
> Allow mousse to chill before attempting to roll into a cylinder.

For The Dressing

Place vinegar, honey and soy sauce in a blender and blitz whilst slowly adding the olive oil. Then add the ginger.

To Serve

Slice mousse, roll in sesame seeds and place on spring onion slices. Arrange orange segments and diced beetroot jelly. Slice duck breast into three slices and place on top. Garnish with micro herbs and dressing.

HERB CRUSTED LOIN OF LOCAL SHROPSHIRE LAMB, CELERIAC GRATIN, PEAS & BROAD BEANS

SERVES 4

Freedom Cross Cinsault Cabernet
(South Africa)

Ingredients

Lamb
1 loin of lamb from the saddle
30g flat leaf parsley
25g rosemary
1 baby shallot
1 clove garlic
100g breadcrumbs
5ml Dijon mustard

Gratin
750g Maris Piper potatoes
350g celeriac
200ml double cream
60g Cheddar cheese
3 cloves garlic
1 sprig rosemary
salt and pepper

Garnish
120g peas and broad beans
4 baby carrots
2 baby parsnips
70g salsify
10g butter

Sauce
lamb stock
450g root vegetables
250ml Madeira
1 tbsp tomato paste
1 sprig rosemary
2 tbsp redcurrant jelly
5g butter
1 bay leaf

Method

For The Lamb

Clean the loin of lamb and *seal* in a hot pan using olive oil until browned. Season and brush with the Dijon mustard

Blend the breadcrumbs with rosemary, chopped shallot and garlic.

Blanch the parsley in boiling water for five seconds then refresh. Squeeze out excess water and blend with the breadcrumbs mix, then roll the sealed lamb in the breadcrumbs evenly. Cook in oven for seven minutes at 165°C.

> **Chef's Tip**
> *Blanching* the parsley makes the breadcrumb mix a brighter green colour.

For The Gratin

Use a mandolin to slice the potatoes and celeriac.

Slowly heat up the cream with the garlic and rosemary until it has been simmering for ten minutes, then strain off.

Layer the potatoes and celeriac, alternating between the two for each layer and seasoning each layer as you go. Then add the cream to cover.

Cover with foil and bake at 180°C for one hour.

Add the cheese and gratinate under the grill.

For The Sauce

Sweat off the root vegetables; add the tomato paste, rosemary, bay leaf and Madeira.

Add the lamb stock until the desired thickness is reached.

Whisk in the redcurrant jelly and *Beurre Monté*, strain and serve.

For The Garnish

Blanch the broad beans for two minutes then add to the peas along with the butter. Cook for two minutes on a low heat and season to taste.

Peel salsify and wash, boil until cooked. Slice at an angle then colour in a pan with butter.

To Serve

Allow the lamb to rest for three minutes then slice into five pieces. Place on top of the broad beans and peas. Arrange the gratin on the plate along with the baby roast parsnip, baby carrot and salsify. Spoon the sauce around the lamb.

TRIO OF CHOCOLATE DESSERT

SERVES 6

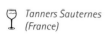 *Tanners Sauternes (France)*

Ingredients

7cm tian rings and 5cm *timbale* moulds

White Chocolate Fondant

100g unsalted butter (plus extra for greasing)
2 tsp icing sugar to dust
100g white chocolate
$^1/_2$ vanilla pod
2 egg yolks
2 whole eggs
100g sugar
100g flour

Chocolate Sabayon

175ml milk
80g chocolate
5 egg yolks
60g sugar
50ml chocolate liqueur
5g white chocolate for grating

Semifreddo Base

15g butter (melted)
1 egg (separated)
25g sugar
25g plain flour
$^1/_2$ tsp baking powder
15g dark chocolate

Semifreddo

300g mascarpone cheese
75g icing sugar
125ml milk
100ml double cream
2 tbsp lemon zest
60g dark chocolate
60g white chocolate
12 raspberries, for garnish
6 sprigs mint

Method

For The Fondant

Butter the *timbale moulds* and dust with icing sugar. Slowly melt the chocolate over simmering water, take off the heat and stir until smooth. Using an electric whisk, mix the egg yolks, the eggs, vanilla and sugar until pale then add this to the chocolate mixture. Sift flour and fold in. Pour into the moulds and oven cook at 160°C for eight minutes.

> **Chef's Tip**
> Use a small knife to turn out fondants and gently shake out.

For The Sabayon

Put the milk into a pan and bring it to a boil. Remove from the heat and melt the chocolate into it.

Using an electric whisk, beat the egg yolks with the sugar and the chocolate milk over a pan of simmering water until the mixture is thick and foamy. Remove from the heat and stir in the liqueur. Pour into glasses and allow to cool before grating the white chocolate over.

For The Semifreddo Base

Line a 18cm x 20cm tray with parchment paper and lightly grease all sides.

Beat egg white until it forms soft peaks. In another bowl beat the egg yolks and sugar until pale and creamy.

Melt the chocolate in a bowl over a pan of simmering water. Mix the flour with the baking powder and sieve into the egg yolk mixture and pour in the melted butter, but don't stir. Add one third of the egg whites and stir. Add the chocolate mix and fold in the remaining egg whites.

Pour into the baking tray and bake for 20 to 25 minutes and then turn out onto a cooling rack.

Cut out rounds using a tian ring.

For The Semifreddo

Mix mascarpone cheese and icing sugar together then stir in the lemon zest and milk.

Whip the cream until stiff and fold into the mascarpone mixture with a whisk. Divide mixture into two portions.

Melt the dark chocolate and pour into one portion of the mascarpone mixture and repeat the process with the white chocolate into the second portion of the mascarpone mixture.

Pour the dark chocolate mixture into a ring to half way and freeze for 20 to 25 minutes. Meanwhile put the white chocolate mixture into a container and freeze also for 20 to 25 minutes.

Once set, add the white chocolate mixture on top of the dark chocolate.

To Serve

Arrange on a plate as per the picture.

050
FISHMORE HALL

Fishmore Road, Ludlow, Shropshire, SY8 3DP

01584 875 148
www.fishmorehall.co.uk

Dating from the late 1800's, Fishmore Hall was originally a family home, but when the Penman family found it, the once magnificent Georgian house had become semi derelict after years of neglect. Reopened in 2007 as a hotel and restaurant following extensive renovations, Fishmore Hall has developed a reputation as one of the UK's up-and-coming venues for fine dining as well as a great place to stay in comfort and contemporary style. Awarded two AA rosettes within weeks of opening, the restaurant, re-named Forelles following the addition of a new orangery extension, earned its third rosette and the hotel's three red stars in 2011 which recognised it as one of the top 200 'Inspector's Choice' establishments in the whole of the UK. Located on the outskirts of Ludlow, a mecca for food lovers, and in the midst of the beautiful rolling South Shropshire countryside, it's hardly surprising that Head Chef David Jaram sources almost everything (except the seafood, of course) from the surrounding area, ensuring the highest quality and freshest ingredients.

With its 15 individually styled bedrooms and designer bathrooms, this is just the place for a romantic weekend getaway or special celebration. It has also become increasingly popular as a perfect venue for weddings and other family gatherings, as well as being ideally placed for out-of-town business meetings and seminars.

Set on a hillside overlooking the historic market town of Ludlow, Fishmore Hall is delighting its guests with fantastic food that has earned its restaurant, Forelles, three AA rosettes. What's more, the hotel has been recognised as an AA Inspectors' Choice, making it one of the best three star hotels in the country.

ROAST QUAIL, FARCED LEG, CORN & CHORIZO

SERVES 4

🍷 *Bourgogne Pinot Noir from Alain Michelot, Bin 406 (France)*

Ingredients

For The Quail

2 whole quail
salt, thyme and garlic (seasoning)
450g duck fat

For The Chicken Mousse

1 chicken fillet
1 egg
200ml double cream
50g caul fat
150g chorizo

4 quail eggs
200g white bread
1 egg (for wash)
plain flour (for coating)

Sweetcorn Purée

250g sweetcorn
250ml double cream
(heat and reduce cream by a third then add
sweetcorn for 5 mins, blitz for 5 mins)

4 baby corn
1 spring cabbage

Method

For The Quail

Remove legs, wishbone and backbone from the quail, leaving the crown, and put to one side. Season legs with salt, thyme and garlic for two hours. Wash and pat dry the legs, place in a small, deep roasting tray with a sheet of greaseproof on the bottom, coat legs with duck fat and cover with another sheet of greaseproof. Place in the oven on 110°C for approximately two hours. Once cooked and the meat is almost falling from the bone, drain and leave to chill until firm. Being careful not to tear the skin, remove the thigh bone from the chilled quail legs by pulling carefully and discard it. Also remove the thigh meat, still keeping the skin intact, and put aside for the farce. Trim the tops of the legs.

For The Chicken Mousse And Farced Leg

Blitz the chicken fillet add one egg then blitz again. Chill for 15 minutes. Beat in 200ml of cream by hand gradually and then season. Dice chorizo into half centimetre cubes (keeping trimmings for breadcrumbs), setting half aside for garnish and put the other half in a mixing bowl. Add two dessert spoons of chicken mousse and chopped thigh meat to the bowl and mix together.

Stuff the thigh with the farce and wrap in caul fat to reform the leg shape, chill until needed.

For The Quail Eggs

For the coating, blitz trimmings of chorizo and bread until they make a rough crumb. Put in a warm, dry place until crisp and blitz again. Place quail eggs in boiling water for approximately two minutes and refresh in iced water. Peel the eggs, roll them in flour, dip into an egg wash and then roll in chorizo breadcrumbs.

Cabbage And Baby Sweetcorn

Blanch the vegetables and refresh in iced water. Pat dry the cabbage leaves and cut into four rectangles of approximately 6cm x 10cm. Finely slice the rest of the cabbage.

Cooking And Finishing

Colour all sides of the quail crown in oil on a medium heat until golden along with the farce leg and baby corn. Remove the baby corn and keep warm. Add a knob of butter and place the quail in oven at 150°C for three and a half minutes. Remove and rest for four minutes before carving the two breasts. Warm the sweetcorn purée and cabbage, panfry the chorizo dice and finish the coated quail egg by deep frying at 165°C for one minute. Arrange a rectangle of cabbage on the base with the sweetcorn purée then stand the leg, place the breast and, using chopped cabbage, make a 'nest' for the quail egg to sit in. Sprinkle over the chorizo to finish.

RABBIT, PEANUT, LIME & TARRAGON

SERVES 4

La Mariana Ouvi Di Ouvi, Bin 223
(Italy)

Ingredients

4 saddle of rabbit and rabbit livers

Ballotine

3 shallots
splash sherry vinegar
sprig of rosemary
16 pancetta slices
100g chicken mousse (see quail recipe)
55g butter
clove garlic

Tarragon Purée

40g tarragon
100g spinach
oil
(Blanch both prepared tarragon and
spinach and refresh. Squeeze excess
water then blitz until smooth)

Tarragon Crumb

40g tarragon
200g white bread
(blitz the above ingredients to form crumbs)

Lime Confit And Jelly

2 x 2 limes
40g lime juice
80g sugar
2g agar agar
125ml water
20g wild mushrooms
peanut butter
12 baby carrots
lemon juice

Method

For The Ballotine

Peel the shallots and colour in a frying pan with a drizzle of oil.
Add rosemary, garlic, 55g butter, a pinch of sugar, salt, pepper and
a splash of sherry vinegar. Roast in the oven at 160°C for
approximately 20 minutes or until soft then leave to cool. Prepare
the rabbit saddle by removing the top end by four bones and split
into two racks of rabbit. French trim the racks. Remove the loin
and fillet from the remaining saddle. On greaseproof paper,
vertically place four slices of pancetta per ballotine, side by side
overlapping each other slightly. Spread the chicken mousse evenly
onto the pancetta. Horizontally across the top of the mousse, from the top
of the mousse furthest away from you, line up the two loins and
place three shallots across the line where the two loins meet.
Then stack the livers on the shallots, season and then place the
rabbit fillets on top. Roll lightly but tightly. Wrap each ballotine in
clingfilm nice and tight and tie the ends to form sausage shapes.

For The Lime Confit

Peel two limes and trim the pith. Slice into thin strips. Place strips
into a pan of cold water and bring to a boil, strain and repeat
four times. With the juice from the two limes, add 40g of sugar
and reduce until sticky, then add the strips and leave to cool.

For The Lime Jelly

Place the lime juice, 40g sugar and 125ml water in a pan, bring
to the boil and leave to cool. Add half of the cooled *liquor* with
the agar agar into another pan and whisk on a high heat until it
reaches boiling point. Remove from heat and add the remaining
half of the *liquor*. Pour into a clingfilm lined container and leave
to set.

For The Baby Carrots

Peel and trim baby carrots, *blanch* in boiling, salted water and
refresh in cold water.

To Finish

Poach ballotine in 75°C water for 15 minutes. Coat rabbit racks
with a little mustard and tarragon crumb. Warm a little peanut
butter and tarragon purée. Warm the baby carrots and spinach in
a little seasoned butter. Remove the ballotine from the clingfilm
and panfry until golden all around and then put in the oven for
four minutes with the coated racks at 160°C. Panfry the
mushrooms with a little seasoning, butter and a few drops of
lemon juice. Paste plate with some of the warm peanut butter,
sprinkle on the tarragon crumb.

To Serve

Slice the ballotine and place onto the plate, using some of the
spinach for support. Add the rack, baby carrots, mushrooms and
tarragon purée. Sprinkle lime jelly, lime *confit* and picked
tarragon to garnish.

TROPICAL FRUIT SALAD, COCONUT SORBET

SERVES 4

Elysium Black Muscat From Alan Quady (USA)

Ingredients

1 pineapple
4 gelatine leaves
100g lychee purée
300g coconut cream
150ml whipping cream
100ml milk
185g sugar
5 passion fruit
1 pomegranate
1 dragon fruit
1 mango
1 watermelon
40g glucose syrup
240ml water

Method

For The Sorbet

Bring the water, 100g sugar and 40g glucose to a boil then leave to cool. Add the coconut cream. Churn in an ice cream machine or place in the freezer, taking it out to whisk occasionally until frozen.

For The Pineapple

Roughly blitz the pineapple in a blender and hang it in muslin cloth to drip overnight, in the fridge if possible.

For The Passion Fruit Jelly

Soak one leaf of gelatine in cold water. Scrape into a saucepan the seeds and juice from passion fruit. Add 55g sugar, 140ml water and boil for approximately five minutes. Strain through sieve and add gelatine. Quarter fill desired mould and leave to set in fridge.

For The Lychee Panna Cotta

Soak three leaves of gelatine. Bring the cream, milk and sugar to the boil in a saucepan then add the gelatine and the lychee purée. Bring back down to room temperature and then add to the mould. Leave to set in the fridge.

> **Chef's Tip**
> To turn the moulds out dip them into a bowl of hot water first to loosen them.

To Garnish

Using a small melon baller scoop 20 balls each out of the mango, watermelon and dragon fruit. Garnish the bowl with five of each of the different fruit balls, adding pomegranate and passion fruit seeds. Place the turned out panna cotta and jelly into the bowl, add sorbet and pour on pineapple juice to finish.

060
THE GRANARY

Heath Lane, Shenstone, Kidderminster, Worcestershire, DY10 4BS

01562 777 535
www.granary-hotel.co.uk

A winning blend of youth and experience is the secret to success for The Granary, a delightful country restaurant in verdant Worcestershire's countryside.

Head Chef Tom Court leads a youthful brigade that put big, rustic dishes on the menu for the venue's discerning diners.

"We have a good team here," says Tom. "Having a settled brigade is a big advantage for us because we are able to grow together."

Tom's ethos is reflected in The Granary's twin AA rosette rating, which it achieved three years ago. "We're delighted to have retained that distinction," says Tom. "Retaining the award recognises the fact that we are at a consistently high standard."

The theme of continuity runs throughout the restaurant. Owner, Richard Fletcher and Head Chef Tom have been working together for ten years.

Tom adds: "Our raison d'etre is local, seasonal produce. We're blessed here to be close to a number of exceptional producers. Our menu is constantly changing to reflect what's available.

"We have brilliant suppliers of meat, great dairies and first class suppliers of fruit and vegetables."

In recent times, The Granary has undergone an extensive refurbishment, so diners can eat in delightful surrounds. A contemporary dining room is complemented by a private dining area, where Tom provides degustation menus.

"The location is great and we aim to please with robust dishes that are classically-inspired," adds Tom.

The Granary's market garden has been producing fruit, vegetables and herbs for three years.

Local horticulturalist Richard Maw oversees the acre plot, to the rear of the restaurant, which ensures produce used in the kitchen is freshly picked.

Granary head chef Tom Court says: "We are incredibly fortunate. We can literally walk out of our kitchen and be in our market garden in 20 seconds. Food doesn't get any fresher or more flavoursome. Our diners can taste the difference."

HAM HOCK & PARSLEY TERRINE, PICCALILLI

SERVES 12

 Mâcon-Vergisson, La Roche Nadine et Maurice Guerrin 2009 (France)

Ingredients

Ham Hock Terrine

2 ham hocks (about 2kg)
1 carrot
2 sticks of celery
1 onion
l leek
2 bay leaves
8 peppercorns
2 star anise
500ml cider or apple juice
100g flat leaf parsley
2 leaves of gelatine (soaked in cold water until soft)

Piccalilli

150g sea salt
1¹/₂ litres water
1kg diced vegetables (onions, celery, fine beans, cauliflower, carrots)
100g gherkins (diced)
500ml cider vinegar
1 star anise
1 bay leaf
10 peppercorns
30g plain flour
¹/₂ tsp turmeric
1 tsp ground ginger
2 tsp English mustard

Chef's Tip

Soak the hocks for 24 hours before cooking to stop the terrine being too salty. Before serving, allow it to stand in room temperature for a little while so that it isn't too cold. Cut it with a very sharp hot knife, or bread knife, to get a clean cut.

Method

For The Ham Hock Terrine

Soak the ham hocks overnight in cold water. That will help stop the terrine being too salty. Roughly cut the carrot, celery, onion and leek, place in a deep ovenproof dish with the ham, bay leaves, peppercorns and star anise. Add the cider and make up with water to cover the hocks.

Cover and cook for between three and a half and four hours in the oven at about 150°C until the meat is soft and falling off the bone. Set aside.

Roughly chop the parsley. Set aside.

Remove the ham hocks from the stock and strain into a saucepan.

Reduce the cooking *liquor* until about 450 to 500ml remains, add the gelatine and taste. Correct the seasoning as required.

Remove all the bones from the hocks and roughly chop the meat.

Mix the chopped ham hock with the parsley and place in a terrine or suitable deep dish.

Pour in the cooking *liquor* to just cover the ham and parsley.

Leave in the refrigerator overnight to set. Dip the terrine dish in hot water for a few seconds and turn out onto a chopping board before serving.

For The Piccalilli

Make brine by combining the sea salt with the warm water. Add all the diced vegetables and gherkins to the brine and leave overnight.

In a saucepan, simmer the cider vinegar with bay leaf, star anise and peppercorns then cover the pan with clingfilm to stop it reducing. Set aside.

In a large bowl mix the English mustard, turmeric, ginger and flour, add a little of the vinegar to make a smooth paste.

Slowly strain the vinegar into the mustard paste, stirring continuously.

Put the mixture into a saucepan and heat over a low heat stirring to stop it going lumpy.

Strain the vegetables out of the brine but do not rinse.

Add the vegetables and simmer for one minute, do not overcook the vegetables - make sure you keep them crisp to give the piccalilli texture. Chill and use as required.

To Serve

Plate as in picture. Serve with toasted rustic bread or ciabatta.

PAN ROAST PORK FILLET ROLLED IN SEED MUSTARD CRUMB, CREAMED POTATOES, STEAMED SPRING GREENS, APPLE FRITTER, CIDER JUS

SERVES 6

Maiden Flight Pinot Noir, Reserva, Casablanca Valley 2010 (Chile)

Ingredients

Pork And Mustard Crumb

white bread (5 slices)
2 tbsp wholegrain mustard
pork tenderloin (approx 1kg)

Creamed Potatoes

1kg potatoes
a pinch of salt
75g butter
100ml double cream

Spring Greens

2 rashers of streaky bacon
3 heads of spring greens
butter

Apple Fritter

100g cornflour
200g plain flour
cold water (approximately 300ml - enough to make a batter)
1 Cox apple

Cider Jus

500ml cider
500ml good stock
redcurrant jelly
butter

Chef's Tip

Rest the tenderloin of pork for ten minutes. Use Nadine or Wilja potatoes for the mash. Use a piping bag for the mash when serving to improve the presentation. Season with salt and pepper - the most important ingredients in the kitchen.

Method

For The Pork And Mustard Crumb

Cover five slices of white bread with wholegrain mustard and leave in a warm oven/hot cupboard until completely dry. This is best done a few days before you need it. Grind in a food processor to a fine crumb. Make sure you keep it dry.

Roll the pork fillet in the mustard crumb, panfry in butter and colour on each side. Place in the oven at 180°C for about ten minutes. Do not overcook or it will be dry. It needs to be slightly pink.

For The Creamed Potatoes

Peel and cut potatoes into even sizes. Bring to the boil with a little salt and cook till soft. Strain and dry the potatoes in the oven for a minute.

First pass the potatoes through a ricer or mandolin. If you want a first class mash then pass again through a fine sieve.

Add butter, cream and season to taste.

For The Spring Greens

Remove all the centre stalks from each leaf and shred as finely as possible. Cut the bacon into fine lardons and fry in a little butter in a saucepan until crisp.

Add the cabbage to the bacon with a little water, cover with a lid and cook for 30 seconds until the cabbage wilts. Season with salt and pepper.

For The Apple Fritter

Mix the cornflour with the flour and add the water slowly to make a thick batter. Core and slice the apple. Dip the apple in the batter and fry in hot oil till golden brown.

For The Cider Jus

Reduce the cider and stock with the redcurrant jelly until it starts to turn to syrup. Remove from the heat and whisk in a little butter to make the sauce shiny and smooth.

To Serve

Plate as in picture. Put the mash in a piping bag and pipe onto the plate. Place the cabbage next to the mash. Carve the pork and place on top. Finish with the fritter and sauce.

RHUBARB & CUSTARD

SERVES 6

🍷 *Muscat De St-Jean-De-Minervois Vignerons De Septimaine 2009 (France)*

Ingredients

Rhubarb

5 sticks of rhubarb
200g caster sugar
400ml white wine
2 star anise
3 strips of citrus fruit peel (orange, lemon or lime)

Sable Biscuits

200g butter (at room temperature)
150g icing sugar
seeds from 1 vanilla pod
2 eggs
400g plain flour

Pastry Cream/Custard

8 egg yolks
100g caster sugar
30g plain flour
4 tsp cornflour
500ml whole milk
1 vanilla pod

Chef's Tip

Use good quality butter to improve the quality of your pastry. Grow your own rhubarb - then you can use only the freshest. Add a little vanilla to the syrup to give it additional flavour. Mark the top of the pastry with a hot skewer.

Method

For The Sable Biscuits

In a large bowl, cream together the soft butter, icing sugar and vanilla until it starts to go pale. Slowly beat in the eggs. Sieve the flour onto the mixture and slowly mix in using your hand until the mixture come together into a ball. Do not overwork the paste.

Chill for 20 minutes before using.

Roll the paste with a little flour to about 3 to 4mm thickness.

Cut into rectangles using a ruler to get them exactly the same size 5cm x 8cm.

Place on greaseproof paper, sprinkle with a little caster sugar before baking at 180°C for about ten minutes, until they start to brown.

For The Pastry Cream/Custard

Cut the vanilla pod down the middle and place in pan with the milk, bring to a boil slowly. In a large bowl, whisk the sugar with the egg yolks till pale, sieve the flour and cornflour in the egg and sugar mixture.

Add the hot milk a little at a time to the eggs and whisk. Place the mixture back on the heat and keep stirring until just before it boils, the mixture will thicken, taste to ensure all the cornflour has cooked out.

Chill the mixture with greaseproof paper on the top to stop it forming a skin. When cold, whisk again till smooth and place in a piping bag with a star nozzle.

For The Poached Rhubarb

In a large saucepan, heat the white wine with the sugar, star anise and citrus fruit peel. Allow to simmer for about 15 minutes to release the flavours into the stock.

Cut the rhubarb into 5cm pieces, place into the stock and remove from the heat.

The rhubarb needs to be just cooked. If you need to put it back on the heat to finish cooking it do so, but do not overcook or it will turn to stewed rhubarb.

Remove the rhubarb from the stock and chill, reduce the stock to a syrup and chill.

To Serve

Dust one biscuit with icing sugar. It will go on top and can be 'scored' with a hot skewer, to create a criss-cross pattern.

Place rhubarb on another biscuit and trim to ensure it is straight. On the other biscuit pipe the pastry cream and place this one on top of the rhubarb. Top with the sugared biscuit and plate with a little of the syrup.

THE HUNDRED HOUSE HOTEL
PUB & RESTAURANT

Bridgnorth Road, Norton, Shropshire, TF11 9EE

01952 580 240
www.hundredhouse.co.uk

The Hundred House Hotel is a Georgian gem and is ideally situated for a trip to Ironbridge or the historic town of Bridgnorth, being just ten minutes from both destinations. The hotel has been owned and run by the Phillips family for 26 years. Head Chef and Managing Partner, Stuart Phillips, has held two AA Rosettes for 17 years, running the restaurant after finishing his training in Michelin star restaurants in France and London. The emphasis here is on the flavours and quality of the food and the menu has been designed to suit everyone's tastes and budget, ranging from bar classics, daily specials and full à la carte menus.

The Hundred House Hotel is a destination for those wanting to 'escape the norm'. You will find no corporate neutrals here, instead you will find character by the bucket load! Roaring fires, dried herbs and flowers hanging from the ceiling, stained glass features throughout, freshly picked flowers from the garden on your table and, most importantly, a very friendly welcome. The restaurant is filled with Sylvia Phillips artwork and interesting antiques and artefacts collected by the family over the years.

Upstairs you will find nine individually styled bedrooms, all having chandeliers, luxurious Victoria and Albert bathroom suites, many with half tester or four poster beds and seven of which have a swing hanging from the oak beams!
Attention to detail such as complimentary filter coffee, bottled water, quality toiletries and lavender scented pillows enhances your stay. The hotel also has stunning and extensive gardens open to the public, as well as over 100 herbs and vegetables growing in the herb garden, which are picked and used by the kitchen on a daily basis.

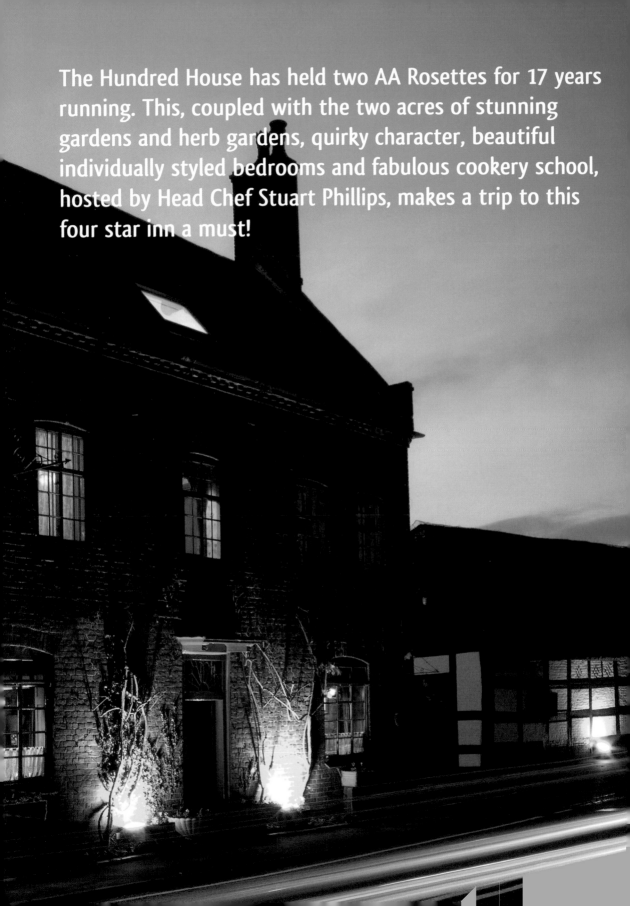

The Hundred House has held two AA Rosettes for 17 years running. This, coupled with the two acres of stunning gardens and herb gardens, quirky character, beautiful individually styled bedrooms and fabulous cookery school, hosted by Head Chef Stuart Phillips, makes a trip to this four star inn a must!

BEETROOT CURED HICKORY SMOKED SALMON

SERVES 4

Alberino Pionero Maccerato. Rias Baixas 2010
(Spain)
Superb smooth well rounded classic dry yet fruity
Spanish wine.

Ingredients

2 x 450g fresh salmon (skinless)
2 beetroot (peeled)
2 oranges (zest and juice)
120g coarse sea salt
120g sugar
60ml dry Martini
hickory (to smoke)

Horseradish Sorbet

450g crème fraiche
285g sugar
570ml water
2 lemons (zest and juice)
170g fresh horseradish (peeled and finely grated)
pinch of salt

Cucumber Ribbons

570ml water
285g sugar
60ml white wine vinegar
1 tbsp fennel seeds
1 cucumber
sorrel to garnish

Method

For The Beetroot

Place the beetroot in a blender and pulse to a purée.
Mix together with orange zest and juice, sugar, salt and Martini.
Roll out a 36 inch sheet of clingfilm on to a table and pour half
of the mix into the centre. Place the salmon on top and then
smother the rest of the mix all over. Wrap the clingfilm tightly
around and place between two trays with a 1kg weight on top.
Refrigerate for 36 hours.

For The Salmon

Remove the salmon from the clingfilm, rinse off the mixture
and pat dry. Cold smoke the salmon for two hours using hickory,
then wrap and put back in fridge.

For The Horseradish Sorbet

Bring the water, sugar and salt to the boil and simmer for five
minutes to make a light syrup, then pour over the horseradish,
add the lemon zest and juice. Leave to infuse overnight.

Mix the syrup with the crème fraiche and churn in an ice cream
machine until set or place in a freezer and stir regularly.

> **Chef's Tip**
> If sorbet is too hard to scoop up, microwave on defrost for
> one to two minutes to make it easier.

For The Cucumber Ribbons

Mix all the ingredients except for the cucumber. Boil and then
simmer for 15 minutes. Peel the skin from the cucumber and
discard, then continue peeling into long strips down to the
seeds. Throw the seeds away and place the cucumber ribbons
into a bowl. Pour the hot sugar and fennel syrup over the
cucumber and refrigerate overnight.

To Serve

Very thinly slice the salmon and place on a plate with twists of
cucumber and springs of fennel and sorrel. Place a scoop of the
horseradish sorbet in the centre and serve immediately with
oatcakes and bread.

ROAST CHUMP OF LAMB WITH PARSNIP, LEEK & LAMB CAKE, CARROT CREAM & ROSEMARY JUS

SERVES 4

Fleurie – Hentri La Fontaine 2008
(France)
Light and subtly soft with hints of wild
raspberries, fruity and delicate with inviting
aromas of cherries and wood smoke.

Ingredients

Lamb

2 x 250g chump of Shropshire lamb
(divided into four portions)
1 sprig rosemary
2 cloves garlic
100ml olive oil

Lamb Cake

200g parsnip (diced and steamed)
200g mashed potato
200g leek
200g lamb shoulder (in pieces)
200g onion (chopped)
50g carrot
50g celery
25g bay leaves, thyme and rosemary
100ml white wine
300ml brown stock
1 lamb kidney (with pith removed)
garlic butter

Carrot Cream

20g carrot
200g swede
200g butter
50g cream
100ml orange
(zest of ¹/₂ orange and juice from a whole)

Method

For The Lamb

Divide the chumps into two and marinade with the oil, garlic and rosemary. Leave overnight to seal in the fridge.

> **Chef's Tip**
>
> We use Shropshire lamb which is very sweet and tasty and the rosemary from our garden makes a huge difference to the cooked flavour. Instead of rosemary, oregano or marjoram from the garden and lemon zest is wonderfully aromatic too.

For The Lamb Cake

In a hot frying pan, brown the piece of lamb shoulder all over, then add the roughly diced vegetables, and place in a hot oven, stirring occasionally until light brown. Add the herbs and wine, boil briefly, then add the stock, cover with foil and bake at 170°C for 90 minutes by which time the lamb will be nice and tender. Remove the lamb and strain off the remaining stock for the lamb *jus*. Cut the leek in half lengthways and *blanch* in boiling water until tender but still bright green. Dice the lamb and mix with the warm parsnip and mash. Season well and shape into cakes. Wrap with the leek and set in the fridge.

For The Carrot Cream

Peel and thinly slice the carrot and swede, then place in a pan with the butter and cook over a low heat with a lid on until soft. Add the orange zest and juice and cook for one minute, then add the cream. Bring to a boil then liquidise until smooth and season.

To Serve

Brown the chump in a hot pan and cook in the oven at 180°C for six to eight minutes. Then leave the meat to rest for five minutes. Sear the lamb kidney in hot oil for one minute (it should still be pink) add garlic butter and leave to rest. Meanwhile, panfry the lamb cakes until golden brown and heat through in the oven. Spoon a swirl of hot carrot cream on the plate, top with the lamb cake, slice the kidney and lamb over and spoon the *jus* around.

(see glossary)
Food Photography by Ross Woodhall

TREACLE TART

SERVES 16

🍷 *Moscatel, Valencia (Spain)*
Very sweet grapey, raisiny, luscious dessert wine.

Method

Line two 10" plates with the pastry, about 2mm thick and raise up the edges leaving to rest in the fridge while you make up the treacle mix.

Remove the crusts and crumb from the loaf, then, placing the crumbs in a bowl, add the syrup, lemon, orange zest and juice. Stir well and divide between the two tart bases.

Use the remaining pastry to create the trellis effect, then bake at 180°C for eight to 12 minutes.

To Serve

Assemble as in picture and serve with vanilla custard.

> **Chef's Tip**
>
> This is the minimum amount to make successfully but it keeps for one week. Bake each portion for four minutes at 180°C, it will be wonderfully crumbly.

Ingredients

1 tin loaf of white bread
2 oranges (zest and juice)
1 lemon (zest and juice)
600g Tate & Lyle golden syrup
750g carefully made sweet shortcrust pastry

080
THE KING & THAI

Avenue Road, Broseley, Shropshire, TF12 5DL

01952 882 004
www.thekingandthai.co.uk

When Suree Coates was named the UK's Best Thai Cook in the 2011 Asian Curry Restaurant Of The Year Awards, few were surprised. After all, the proprietor of Broseley's King And Thai restaurant has spent a lifetime honing her skills as a chef.

Suree learned to cook as a five-year-old, watching her grandmother make complicated flavourings, pastes and sauces. "My grandmother was the first person to teach me," she says.

"Everything was always fresh, including the herbs and the spices" she explains. The youthful Suree would set the family fire and spend many hours pounding on a pestle and mortar. Suree's father would bring fish from the river and she would harvest locally grown vegetables.

She moved to the UK 20 years ago and opened the King And Thai with her partner, Simon Turner, creating an intimate neighbourhood bistro in picturesque Ironbridge before relocating to the nearby market town of Broseley.

Suree's restaurant is ideally situated in the beautiful Shropshire countryside, where there are ample supplies of high quality meat, fresh vegetables and summer fruits. Suree also makes regular 3am trips to Birmingham Fish Market, to obtain catches from day boats.

Suree is also one of the Midlands' finest pastry chefs, a self-taught artisan who specialises in extravagantly pretty dishes. Spending hours on good presentation, she is a past master at shaping chocolate, carving fruit and fusing the best of Asian and British desserts.

"I like guests to enjoy the wow factor when they eat here," she adds. Her guests agree, describing her desserts as 'art on a plate'.

Suree favours traditional Thai dishes that offer stunning, fragrant flavours. She balances sour and sweet, salty and bitter, savoury and mild. Her restaurant avoids fads, sticking to traditional Thai dishes like red and green curries and pad thai. Coconut dishes are infused with delicate ingredients like crushed coriander, a hint of fresh lime, ginger, chilli and fresh turmeric. "Thai cooking is all about great flavour combinations," says Suree. "We offer food that is light, fresh and very palatable."

THAI FISH THREE WAYS, WASABI SAUCE

SERVES 4

Andre Dezat Pouilly Fume 2008/2009
(France)

Ingredients

For The Fish

1 x 350g portion salmon fillet
1 x 350g portion sea bass fillet
1 x 350g portion mackerel fillet
small packet dried seaweed (to coat the outside
of the mackerel)

Marinade

150ml rice wine vinegar
1 tbsp granulated sugar
2 large red chillies (deseeded)
2 tbsp fish sauce
1 clove garlic
2 tsp light soy sauce
1 stick dill (to garnish)

Wasabi Sauce

4 tbsp homemade mayonnaise
1 tsp wasabi paste
1 tbsp double cream
1 tbsp cooking oil
1 slice bread (brown)

Method

For The Fish

De-bone the fish, or alternatively you could ask your fishmonger to do it for you. Now, take each piece of fish and slice it very thinly. You are looking for slices no more than 5mm thick.

Set the three different fish aside in individual bowls and leave to chill.

Now Start On Your Marinades

Combine all ingredients for the marinade in the same bowl. Pour the marinade into each of the three fish bowls and leave to infuse for 30 minutes. Do not leave the marinade for any longer. The object is to give the fish the flavour of the sauce but if you leave it for too long the marinade will mask the flavour of the fish. The vinegar in the marinade will also overcook the fish if you leave it for too long.

Now You Need To Cook The Mackerel

First, pat the dried seaweed against the mackerel so as to coat the outside. Now pour a little vegetable oil into a hot frying pan and cook through. An option is to serve the mackerel in a toasted bread cone.

To make the bread cone, simply wrap a slice of bread around a rolling pin and put in an oven at 180°C for five minutes. It will retain its cone shape when cooled.

Wasabi Sauce

Put the homemade mayonnaise, wasabi paste and one tablespoon of double cream into a bowl and add one tablespoon of cooking oil. Mix the ingredients together until they are well combined. It should be a runny paste. Set aside.

To Serve

Plate as seen in picture.

Place on a rectangular-shaped plate, if you have one.

Lie the sea bass together in thin strips at one end. They should overlap one another.

For the salmon, roll the strips together using clingfilm to form a rose shape. Place upright on the centre of the plate and serve up the wasabi paste beside this. You can garnish with micro leaves or salad.

Place the mackerel nests at the end of the plate.

> **Chef's Tip**
> Make sure the fish is very fresh. Look at its scales and eyes glistening.

MONKFISH & KING PRAWN THAI GREEN CURRY, VEGETABLES, FRAGRANT RICE

SERVES 4

🍷 *Cave de Turckheim Gewürztraminer 2009/10*
(Alsace, France)

Ingredients

Monkfish And King Prawn Thai Green Curry

4 x approx 250g monkfish tails (skinned
and deboned)
12 large, fresh king prawns (de-veined)

Green Curry Paste

1 tbsp fish sauce
1 tbsp sugar
200ml coconut cream
2 stalks lemongrass
4 shallots (finely chopped)
5 cloves of garlic (chopped)
3 large green chillies
$1/2$ tbsp galangal (ginger is a good alternative)
1 tsp shrimp paste
$1/2$ tsp black peppercorns
50g bamboo shoots
50g Thai aubergine

Fragrant Rice

250g Tilda Thai jasmine rice
375ml water

Method

For The Green Curry

Bash the lemongrass, shallots, garlic, green chillies, galangal, shrimp paste and peppercorns together with a pestle and mortar.

Then add 50ml of cooking oil to a hot pan. Add the green curry ingredients and fry off the paste.

Now add one tablespoon of fish sauce and one tablespoon of sugar to the pan. Then add the 200ml of coconut cream.

Next add the vegetables and cook until tender. You should be able to cook them within two or three minutes.

Now add the fish. The monkfish should cook through in four or five minutes, so that it is white through. The prawns will take a little less time. You will know they are cooked when they turn pink. The curry will simmer as the fish cooks. Then, when the fish is done, remove from the heat.

For The Fragrant Rice

Simply steam the rice for around 15 minutes, until tender and soft.

To Serve

Place the rice in a *timbale* then plate up in a large-sized dinner bowl, or round plate, and place the monkfish on top of the rice. Then stack the prawns on top of the monkfish. Then swoosh the green curry around the side of rice and fish.

> **Chef's Tip**
> Decorate the prawns with crispy vermicelli noodles if you want to add a little pizzazz.

MANGO TART, STICKY THAI COCONUT RICE PUDDING, MANGO ROSE

SERVES 4

 Brown Brothers Special Late Harvested Orange Muscat and Flora (Australia)

Ingredients

Coconut Rice Pudding

100g Thai sticky rice
200ml coconut milk
50g sugar
1 tsp salt
1 tbsp cornflour
1 tbsp white sesame seed
1 tbsp black sesame seed

Mango Rose

1 ripe mango

Mango Tart

1 ripe mango
1 batch sweet pastry (12 x 10cm circles)
100ml mango purée
4 egg yolks
100ml double cream
50g caster sugar

Method

For The Coconut Rice Pudding

For the best results, wash, then steam your rice for around 90 minutes, preferably in a steamer. Add the coconut milk and the sugar to a heavy-bottomed pan. Alternatively, you can add the rice, sugar and coconut milk together in the heavy-bottomed pan and boil gently until soft.

When the rice is cooked, add salt and cornflour. Mix the ingredients together and set aside. The cornflour will make the mixture very thick and sticky. Leave to one side.

The rice will be so firm that it can be cut with a knife. Cut into the shapes you would like - circles or squares - then dip into the different coloured sesame seeds, to decorate.

For The Mango Tart

Purée the mango in a blender at the highest speed.

Make a batch of sweet pastry for the tart cases or buy this ready made. The pastry needs to chill for at least an hour, or better still, overnight. If you do not have time, you can freeze for 15 to 30 minutes until very cold but not frozen. Fill a muffin case tray with 10cm circles of the sweet pastry and bake blind at 180°C until golden brown. That should take about 12 to 15 minutes. Leave to cool.

Now Make Your Filling

Take the mango purée and add the four egg yolks, double cream and 50g of caster sugar. You are effectively making mango custard.

Place those ingredients in a heavy-bottomed pan and warm on a moderate heat. Do not boil - that will scramble the eggs and ruin your mixture. The mixture should coat the back of a spoon. Continue to stir throughout, to make sure the consistency is glossy and even. Leave to rest in the fridge for 30 minutes. Now fill the tart cases with the mango custard. Decorate with small 5cm dice made from the remaining mango.

For The Flower

Slice the mango as thin as is possible. Place the strips on clingfilm, so that they are slightly overlapped. Now roll them together, gently removing the clingfilm. When you remove the final strip of clingfilm you will have a rose shape.

To Serve

Plate as in picture.

Chef's Tip

You can also make a more elaborate dessert by making a passion fruit purée, which goes beneath one of the elements.

090
LA BÉCASSE

17 Corve Street, Ludlow, Shropshire, SY8 1DA

01584 872 325
www.labecasse.co.uk

Chef patron - Will Holland
Sous chef - James Walshaw (pictured picking wild garlic)
Restaurant manager - Chris Grobelny
Assistant restaurant manager/sommelier - Genaro Effuso (wine choices)

La Bécasse Restaurant, situated in the historic medieval market town of Ludlow, opened its doors in 2007. It was soon acknowledged to be one of the best restaurants in the country, quickly picking up a string of accolades and coveted awards. Owned by Alan Murchison of L'otolan Restaurant fame, La Bécasse is run by chef patron Will Holland who prides himself on offering an array of exciting and original menus in a unique setting.

La Bécasse Restaurant consists of a series of intimate dining rooms - some with historic oak panelling, others with exposed stone walls. A secluded courtyard provides the perfect place for an aperitif and on the first floor is a cosy oak-beamed Champagne bar. Stylish, contemporary touches complement the original features of the listed, 17th Century former coaching inn which houses the restaurant. The restaurant staff aim to provide a friendly, knowledgeable and unintimidating service.

Chef Will Holland has always had a passion for cooking and never wanted to be anything other than a chef. He worked for over a decade in some of the country's finest Michelin-starred restaurants and hotels before taking on the challenge of opening and running La Bécasse. He describes the style of the food he serves as a modern British interpretation of classic dishes. He is a keen supporter of locally produced food and prides himself on having great relationships with nearby farmers, other food producers and suppliers.

'As a chef, I believe it is my duty to give the ingredients that enter my kitchen the respect they deserve by preparing and cooking them to the very best of my ability'. Chef Will Holland, Ludlow 2012.

PIGEON CARPACCIO, MANGO SALSA, SESAME, WASABI, RED WINE REDUCTION

SERVES 4

 Josmeyer, Pinot Gris, 2008, Alsace, Le Fromenteau (France)

Ingredients

Pigeon Carpaccio

50g demerara sugar
5g dried orange zest
4 wood pigeon breasts

Mango Salsa

1 mango
1 red chilli
2 spring onions
1 lime
12 sprigs coriander

Red Wine And Sesame Reduction

1125ml red wine
25g sugar
20ml toasted sesame oil

Sweet And Sour Papaya Purée

185g fresh papaya flesh
50g sugar
30ml white wine vinegar
7ml lime juice
18g vegi gel

Crispy Leek

1 leek
20g cornflour

Additional Ingredients/Elements

foie gras terrine
toasted sesame seeds
wasabi paste
coriander cress

Chef's Tip

The pigeon appears to be raw but in fact it is cooked due to the low temperature it is poached at. You can cook many other meats using the same technique to retain their colour and 'raw' appearance.

Method

For The Pigeon Carpaccio

Place the sugar and dried orange zest in a food processor and grind into a powder. Sprinkle the pigeon breasts with the powder. Roll each pigeon breast tightly in clingfilm and tie each end to form sausage shapes. Poach the pigeon 'sausages' in a water bath at 45°C for one hour. Plunge the cooked pigeons into iced water for ten minutes before transferring to the freezer until required. 30 minutes before serving, remove the pigeons from the freezer, remove and discard the clingfilm and thinly slice.

For The Mango Salsa

Peel and dice the mango into 5mm cubes. Remove the seeds from the chilli and finely dice. Finely dice the spring onion. Remove the zest from the lime using a fine grater. Juice the lime after the zest has been removed. Pick the leaves from the coriander and finely chop discarding the stalks. Place all the prepared ingredients in a bowl. Season with salt and sugar to taste and mix. Store in the refrigerator until required.

For The Red Wine And Sesame Reduction

Place the red wine and sugar in a saucepan and reduce over a medium heat until 75ml remains. Whisk in the sesame oil. Transfer the *reduction* to a small plastic squeezy bottle and retain at room temperature until required.

For The Sweet And Sour Papaya Purée

Place all the ingredients in a liquidiser and blend until smooth. Transfer the purée into a saucepan. Bring to the boil over a high heat stirring continuously. Pour the cooked purée into a container and place in the refrigerator until set and cold. Return the set purée back into the liquidiser and blend until smooth. Pass the purée through a fine sieve and store in a plastic squeezy bottle in the refrigerator until required.

For The Crispy Leek

Use only the white part of the leek. Slice the leek into fine strips. Place in a bowl with the cornflour and mix. Deep fry the prepared leek at 140°C for approximately one minute or until crispy and lightly golden in colour. Season lightly with salt and shape into 'nests'. Store on absorbent kitchen paper at room temperature until required.

To Finish And Assemble The Dish

Cut the foie gras terrine into 1cm thick slices and stamp into rings using warmed pastry cutters. Coat the cut sides of the foie gras rings with toasted sesame seeds. Assemble as in the picture using a pastry brush to 'paint' the wasabi onto the plate and garnishing the dish with coriander cress.

BRAISED ROSÉ VEAL SHANK, OCTOPUS, FENNEL SALAD, CARROTS

SERVES 4

 Echezeaux, Grand Cru 2003, Domaine René Engel (France)

Ingredients

Braised Veal Shanks

2 x 900g whole English rosé veal shanks
1 clove garlic
1 sprig thyme
1 bay leaf
6 black peppercorns

Octopus Carpaccio

1 x 850g whole fresh octopus

Carrot And Orange Purée

400g carrots
450ml freshly squeezed orange juice
1 sprig rosemary
250ml light olive oil

Pickled Carrot Ribbons

70ml white wine vinegar
50ml white wine
60ml water
60g sugar
20ml freshly squeezed orange juice
2 carrots

Additional Ingredients/Elements

blanched baby carrots (tops on)
chopped curly parsley
shaved raw fennel
thinly sliced kumquat
red vein sorrel cress

Chef's Tip

Cooking and preparing veal in this way is a refined version of 'osso buco' without serving it on the bone. The shank is an affordable and accessible cut of English rosé veal which can be expensive for the more prime cuts.

Method

For The Braised Veal Shanks

Place the veal shanks in a large vacuum pack bag with the other ingredients. Seal the bag on full vacuum. Place the bag of veal shanks in a water bath at 62°C for 72 hours. Remove the bag from the water bath and open. Remove the cooked veal shanks and reserve any cooking juices. Carefully remove the natural 'lobes' of meat from the shanks. Discard all bones and fat. Place the cooked veal shank lobes in an ovenproof dish, add the reserved cooking juices, cover and keep warm. Before serving glaze under a medium heat grill.

For The Octopus Carpaccio

Remove the tentacles from the octopus and discard the body. Wash the tentacles thoroughly under cold running water until they are clean and completely free from ink. Roll all the tentacles tightly together in clingfilm so they are running parallel to each another and tie each end to form a sausage shape. Poach the octopus 'sausage' in a waterbath at 85°C for four hours. Plunge the cooked octopus into iced water for ten minutes before transferring to the freezer until required. 30 minutes before serving, remove the octopus from the freezer, remove and discard the clingfilm and thinly slice. When it comes to serving, placing the carpaccio onto warmed plates will be enough to reheat the octopus sufficiently.

For The Carrot And Orange Purée

Peel and finely chop the carrots. Place them in a saucepan with the orange juice and rosemary. Cook uncovered over a high heat until the carrots are tender and the orange juice has reduced until syrupy. Remove and discard the rosemary before transferring the orange syrup and cooked carrot to a liquidiser. Add the oil and blend until smooth. Season with salt and sugar to taste. Pass the purée through a fine sieve and store in a plastic squeezy bottle at room temperature until required.

For The Pickled Carrot Ribbons

Place all the ingredients apart from the carrots into a saucepan and bring to the boil. Remove from the heat. Thinly slice the carrots lengthways into ribbons using a Japanese mandolin. Add the carrot ribbons to the warm *liquor* and leave to pickle for a minimum of 30 minutes. To serve roll the carrot ribbons into tubes.

To Finish And Assemble The Dish

Roll the blanched baby carrots in the chopped parsley. Assemble as in the picture using the fennel, kumquat and sorrel as a salad along the top of the braised veal shank.

GINGER & LIME JELLY, MAPLE PARFAIT, HICKORY SMOKED FOAM, GINGER BISCUIT

SERVES 4

Vigna Del Volta, 2007, Emilia, Malvaisa Passito
(Italy)

Ingredients

Ginger And Lime Jelly

4 leaves bronze leaf gelatine
500ml ginger beer
100ml freshly squeezed lime juice
50g sugar
2 limes
50g candied stem ginger
12 mint leaves

Maple Parfait

100g whole egg
120g egg yolk
125g maple syrup
175g sugar
50ml water
500ml double cream

Hickory Smoked Foam

2 leaves bronze leaf gelatine
50g sugar
150ml ginger beer
100g maple syrup
325ml hickory smoked water
25ml lime juice

Ginger Biscuit

55g unsalted butter
30g demerara sugar
85g golden syrup
115g plain flour
3g bicarbonate of soda
6g ground ginger

Chef's Tip

An iced parfait makes a great alternative to ice cream
if you don't have an ice cream machine, as it doesn't
require churning. It can be frozen in individual dishes
or moulds or in a larger freezer proof container and
scooped as with conventional ice cream.

Method

For The Ginger And Lime Jelly

Soak the gelatine in cold water. Place the ginger beer, sugar and
lime juice in a saucepan and warm over a low heat until the sugar
has dissolved. Remove from the heat. Remove the gelatine from
the water and squeeze it of any excess water before adding it to
the pan to dissolve. Remove the skin from the limes using a knife
and remove the segments. Finely dice the ginger and mint.
Divide the lime segments, ginger and mint between four glasses.
Divide the liquid jelly between the glasses and transfer them to
the refrigerator to set and store until required.

For The Maple Parfait

Whisk the egg and egg yolk in an electric mixer until light and
pale in colour. Meanwhile, place 50g of the maple syrup, 100g of
the sugar and the water into a saucepan and boil to form a syrup.
Gradually add the boiling syrup into the whisked egg while the
mixer is continuously whisking. Place the remaining maple syrup
and sugar in a saucepan and place over a high heat until a dark
caramel is formed. Remove the pan from the heat and carefully
deglaze the caramel by adding 100ml of the double cream. Add
this caramel cream to the egg mixture, mix together and place in
the refrigerator to allow to cool. Semi whip the remaining double
cream. Fold the whipped cream into the cooled mixture and pour
into a freezer proof container. Freeze until required.

For The Hickory Smoked Foam

Soak the gelatine in cold water. Place the remaining ingredients
in a saucepan and warm over a low heat until the sugar and
syrup has dissolved. Remove from the heat. Remove the gelatine
from the water and squeeze it of any excess water before adding
it to the pan to dissolve. Transfer the liquid into a cream whipper
siphon gun. Assemble the whipper correctly and charge with
three gas cartridges. Store in the refrigerator until required.
Shake vigorously before using.

For The Ginger Biscuit

Soften the butter. Add the sugar and golden syrup to the soft
butter and beat until smooth. Add the remaining ingredients and
mix until the biscuit dough is formed. Do not overwork the dough
at this stage. Place the dough between two sheets of silicone
paper and roll until 2mm thick. Rest the rolled biscuit dough in
the refrigerator for 30 minutes. Bake the biscuit dough in an oven
at 150°C for eight to ten minutes or until golden. Whilst warm
cut the biscuit into 5mm strips. Crush the remaining biscuit into a
coarse crumb. Store the biscuits and crumb in an airtight
container until required.

To Finish And Assemble The Dish

Assemble as in the picture using an ice cream scoop to ball the
maple parfait.

100
LION & PHEASANT

50 Wyle Cop, Shrewsbury, SY1 1XJ

01743 770 345
www.lionandpheasant.co.uk

The phrase 'well-travelled' was invented for chefs like Matthew Strefford, the cook who leads the kitchen at Shrewsbury's Lion And Pheasant Hotel, who flew around the world in search of inspiration before returning to his home county.

In Australia, he spent time alongside Neil Perry, known as 'The King Of Modern Dining', working at a number of restaurants including The Rockpool, Perry's flagship fine dining restaurant.

He also impressed during a stint at the five-star luxury castle hotel Adare Manor in County Limerick, Ireland, which is well known for its international business community clientele.

Matthew says: "I enjoyed travelling, living in different parts of the world and learning about different flavours and different combinations. I spent some years on the road and would happily have continued.

The only thing that could have brought me back was becoming head chef at my home town's best restaurant. I was delighted, therefore, when I was offered that post at the Lion And Pheasant."

The Lion And Pheasant Hotel in Wyle Cop, Shrewsbury has been praised from all quarters since its doors were opened in November 2010. It has been named one of the UK's top ten boutique hotels, with diners luxuriating amid décor that is fresh and contemporary.

The Tudor townhouse hotel has an elegant interior in which Strefford offers dishes inspired by the flavours of contemporary Britain, France, Asia and Italy.

"I love being back in Shropshire," Matthew adds. "I grew up on a farm, so this county has strong associations for me."

The best of local cuisine features daily on Matthew Strefford's menu. The head chef at the Lion And Pheasant grew up on a farm and spends his spare time hunting out new ingredients or suppliers. "Growing up in a farming family, I have a lot of respect for farmers and for their produce. I want to bring a lot of local produce into my menus. It is all about flavour for me and working with the wonderful flavours and ingredients that can be found in Shropshire and the Welsh coast."

PANFRIED DUCK LIVERS & MAYNARD'S BLACK PUDDING, FREE RANGE DUCK EGG, WATERCRESS SALAD

SERVES 6

🍷 *Fleurie, André Cologne 2009 (France)*

Ingredients

Duck Livers

12 duck livers
25ml sherry vinegar
6 free range duck eggs
400g black pudding

Salad

300g watercress (washed and picked)
lemon juice and olive oil

Dressing

6 shallots (peeled and very finely diced)
250ml red wine
1 tbsp red wine vinegar
1 tbsp sugar
salt and pepper
dash of rapeseed oil

Method

For The Duck Livers With Black Pudding And Duck Egg

Trim duck livers of any fat, veins and sinew then pat dry and set aside.

Slice black pudding into 1cm rounds.

Fry eggs in one frying pan. At the same time, heat up a second and fry the black pudding and livers, ensuring the livers remain pink. *Deglaze* the pan with the sherry vinegar and set aside.

For The Salad And Dressing

Make the dressing by putting the diced shallots in a pan with the red wine. Reduce until syrupy and all wine has evaporated. Season to taste with vinegar, sugar, salt and pepper, cover with the rapeseed oil.

Dress the watercress with the lemon juice and olive oil.

> **Chef's Tip**
>
> If you can find wild watercress, use it. It grows in abundance in streams on the outskirts of Shrewsbury and has a wonderful peppery flavour.

To Serve

Arrange the eggs in the middle of a warmed plate and scatter the livers and black pudding around the outside. Now stack the dressed salad on the side. Drizzle the shallot dressing over the top of the salad dressing and serve immediately.

ROAST LOIN OF LAMB, CRISPY BELLY, SWEETBREADS, JERUSALEM ARTICHOKE PUREE & GARLIC

SERVES 6

 *Montagny 1er Cru, Louis Latour 2009
(France)*

Ingredients

For The Lamb

¹/₂ saddle of lamb, including the belly
12 lamb sweetbreads

Confit Oil

5 shallots
6 cloves garlic
a few sprigs thyme
a few sprigs rosemary
6 black peppercorns
3 bay leaves
peeled zest of 1 lemon
sea salt

Artichoke Purée

150g butter
200g shallots
800g Jerusalem artichokes
2 cloves garlic
2 sprigs thyme
400ml chicken stock
200ml double cream

Vegetables

200g wild garlic (stalks removed,
lowers set aside)

Garlic Mash

10 cloves garlic
1kg floury potatoes
150g butter
150ml whole milk

Chef's Tip

This recipe requires basic butchery techniques.
Don't be afraid to try at home but if in doubt ask
your butcher to prepare the meat for you.

Method

For The Lamb

Remove the loin and belly from the saddle, separate the loin
from the belly and trim off any sinew. Cut into six equal portions
about 150g each.

Season the belly well with salt and pepper and add to a tray with
the vegetables. Cover with oil, seal the tray with foil and cook at
120°C for about three and a half hours, until the fat has
rendered out of the meat and the meat is wonderfully tender.

Carefully remove from the oven and press the meat between two
trays to achieve a flat shape. Set aside to cool.

Blanch the sweetbreads for one minute then peel off any fat and
sinew, pat dry and set aside.

When the belly has cooled, cut it into 3cm x 8cm fingers.

When you are ready to eat, season all your meat and *seal* off the
loin in a hot pan. Then cook in the oven at 180°C for six to eight
minutes for medium rare. In the same pan, *seal* off the belly and
sweetbreads to give a good brown crust. Leave to rest for a few
minutes with the loin.

Deglaze the pan with lamb stock and reduce the liquid to a
good, silky consistency.

For The Artichoke Purée, Garlic Mash And Wild Garlic

Make the purée by sweating the artichokes, shallots, garlic and
thyme in butter until soft but without colour. Now add chicken
stock and reduce by half. Then add cream, reduce again and blitz.
Season to taste.

Boil the garlic cloves from cold then refresh. Repeat three times
then crush to a purée.

Boil the potatoes in salted water, drain well then mash and beat
them in the warm milk, butter and garlic purée, season to taste.

Wilt the wild garlic in some butter. Warm up the mash and
artichoke purée and adjust the seasoning.

To Serve

Arrange the mash, purée and garlic on a warm plate. Carve the
lamb and place on the garlic, with the sweetbreads and belly.
Garnish with garlic flowers, parsley shoots and the sauce.

VALRHONA CHOCOLATE & RASPBERRY MOELLEUX, PISTACHIO TUILLE & MASCARPONE MOUSSE

SERVES 6

🍷 *Stanton and Killeen, Rutherglen Muscat (Australia)*

Ingredients

Moelleux

200g Valrhona Manjari chocolate 64% solids
200g unsalted butter
200g caster sugar
200g whole eggs
45g plain flour

Tuille

50g icing sugar
50g plain flour
50g butter
50g melted butter
1 tbsp pistachios

Mascarpone Mousse

75g egg yolks
115g sugar
3 leaves fine gelatine
570g mascarpone
300ml double cream
1 vanilla pod
150g fresh raspberries
60ml Framboise liqueur

Method

For The Chocolate And Raspberry Molleux

Melt the butter and chocolate together in a *bain-marie* and set it aside.

Whisk the sugar and eggs on a high speed in a mixer for ten minutes.

Fold the egg and sugar into the chocolate and butter, then sift in the flour and slowly fold in until fully incorporated. Put in a container and set aside.

Steep the raspberries in the Framboise.

Place macerated raspberries in the bottom of a ramekin or bowl. Spoon moelleux mix over the top and bake for five to six minutes. A slight wobble indicates a nice gooey centre.

Remove from oven leave to rest for one minute.

For The Tuille

To make the *tuille* beat together the egg whites, sugar and flour to form a paste then beat in melted butter.

Make a template using the lid of an old ice cream container to cut out a long teardrop shape. Spread the *tuille* mix thinly over the template on a *Silopat* mat. Sprinkle chopped pistachios over the top and bake for six to eight minutes until golden brown. Remove from oven and curve around a wine bottle to set. Leave to cool.

For The Mascarpone Mousse

For the mousse, soak the gelatine leaves in cold water until soft. Then whip the cream and mix with the mascarpone and the vanilla.

Whisk the egg yolks until light and fluffy. Boil sugar to 118°C then pour the hot sugar over whisked eggs and whisk in the gelatine. Mix the eggs with mascarpone mix. Fill ramekins or small bowls and chill to set.

To Serve

Dust the molleux with icing sugar, place the *tuille* on the mousse, garnish with fresh raspberries and serve at once.

> **Chef's Tip**
>
> This dish works equally well with cherries instead of raspberries. If you can't find Valrhona, substitute it with another good quality dark chocolate.

110
THE LION
AT BREWOOD

1 Market Place, Brewood, Staffordshire, ST19 9BS

01902 850 123
www.lionhotelbrewood.co.uk

Head chef Philip Olivant spent more years than he cares to remember trawling the globe in search of culinary adventures. Working in numerous locations, including a four year stint in the Cayman Islands, taught him about different flavours, techniques and combinations.

But the Stone-born cook always hankered for a return to his native Staffordshire and in 2011 fulfilled that dream by becoming the head chef at The Lion.

"I spent a lot of years working around the world," he says, "but I always wanted to come home. Staffordshire is one of UK's most under rated counties. We have a history of brilliant, flavoursome food. We've got great meat, game, vegetables, fruit and cloth-bound cheeses on our doorstep."

Philip's robust flavours have proved a hit at The Lion, one of Shropshire's most historic hotel-restaurants. He is upholding a tradition for good food that dates back many generations. The 18th Century, Grade II Listed property was formerly two separate hostelries: The Giffard Arms and The Red Lion.

They were run by different proprietors until 1850, when they were combined into one establishment. Good food continued down the years and during one period in The Lion's history it operated as one of Staffordshire's most exclusive hotels.

"We've got a beautiful dining room, with plenty of exposed oak beams," adds Philip. "The venue really complements the food. We cook with the seasons.

We're proud of our Terroir and we aim to do it justice through imaginative but hearty dishes."

Award-winning produce from local suppliers features heavily on the menu at The Lion. Chef Philip Olivant says: "We're all about seasonal, fresh and local. Our grocer even pops in every morning to tell us what he's got." Staffordshire has high quality producers, like rape seed oil maker Just Oils, and many more besides. "It's an incredible area and we live off the land," adds Philip. The county also has an impressive network of independent retailers and farm shops, stocking locally produced food and drink.

POTTED CRAB, CHORIZO BUTTER, FENNEL & ORANGE SALAD

SERVES 4

Chablis 2010 Cave des Vignerons de Chablis, Burgundy (France)

Ingredients

Potted Crab

100g white crab meat
100g brown crab meat
5g coriander (finely chopped)
$^1/_2$ lime (finely grated zest and juice)
20g crème fraîche
1 small banana shallot (finely diced)
1 tsp chives (finely chopped)
1 tbsp olive oil
Tabasco sauce to taste
fish sauce (nam pla) to taste
25g butter (melted)
10g chorizo (finely diced)
salt and pepper

Fennel And Orange Salad

1 large orange (segmented)
1 fennel bulb (finely shaved)
pinch smoked paprika
2 tbsp vinaigrette

Toast

4 slices white bread

Method

For The Potted Crab

Sauté shallot and chorizo lightly in olive oil until softened, add melted butter and leave to infuse for 15 minutes. Now stir in chives then set aside.

Mix the brown crab meat with a third of the coriander, a half of the lime juice and zest, a dash of tabasco, a dash of fish sauce and season with salt and pepper. Set aside.

Now mix the white crab meat with the remaining lime juice and lime zest, a third of the coriander, crème fraîche, a dash of tabasco, a dash of fish sauce and season with salt and pepper.

Now spoon the brown crab mix into the bottom of four glasses, top with the white crab mix and top with the chorizo butter. Refrigerate.

For The Fennel And Orange Salad

Mix fennel, the remaining coriander, orange segments, smoked paprika, vinaigrette and leave for three to four minutes. Toss lightly, so as to coat all elements before serving.

For The Toast

Toast bread, remove crusts and cut into diamond shapes before serving.

To Serve

Plate as in picture.

> **Chef's Tip**
>
> This dish is all about balance. So taste, taste, taste as you go. Don't be heavy handed with the Tabasco, fish sauce or other seasons. Keep on tasting to get the balance right.

SEA TROUT, SPROUTING BROCCOLI, NEW POTATOES & SAUCE VIERGE

SERVES 4

🍷 *D'Arenberg The Hermit Crab Viognier Marsanne (Australia)*

Ingredients

Sea Trout And Vegetables

4 x 170g portions sea trout
400g sprouting broccoli
200g new potatoes

Sauce Vierge

100ml extra virgin olive oil
1 lemon (juice only)
2 tomatoes (skins and seeds removed, finely chopped)
1 shallot (finely chopped)
1 small garlic clove (finely chopped)
2 tbsp fresh tarragon (roughly chopped)
2 tbsp fresh basil (roughly chopped)
2 tbsp fresh dill (roughly chopped)
salt and freshly ground black pepper to season

Method

For The Sea Trout And Vegetables

Lightly oil and place sea trout skin side down in a non-stick pan on medium heat and leave until you see the flesh changing colour around the edges and nearly to the top.

You should achieve a pleasant orange-pink colour and when you press your thumb against the top of the fillet, it should 'give'.

Trim and boil the potatoes in salted water until tender, toss with a little butter and season. The size of the potatoes will determine the time it takes to cook them. Test by pushing a sharp knife through. When they are cooked, the potatoes will not resist the knife.

Trim and boil sprouting broccoli in salted water for a few minutes until tender. Toss with a little butter and season.

> **Chef's Tip**
> Score the skin with a sharp knife to assist the cooking and prevent it curling up.

For The Sauce Vierge

This should be prepared before you cook the sea trout and vegetables. Simply combine all ingredients, adjust the seasoning, then refrigerate.

To Serve

Assemble the dish as in picture.

VANILLA PANNA COTTA, STRAWBERRY COMPOTE, RASPBERRY SORBET, PRALINE CRISP

SERVES 4

🍷 *Tabali Encantado Late Harvest Muscat 2009/10*
Limari Valley (Sweet) (Chile)

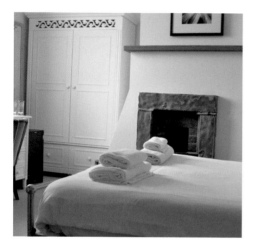

Ingredients

Panna Cotta

400ml double cream
60ml milk
1 gelatine leaf
20g sugar
1 vanilla pod

Strawberries

200g strawberries
icing sugar (to coat strawberries)

Raspberry Sorbet

40g caster sugar
10ml water
225g fresh, good quality raspberries
1 tsp lemon juice

Praline

50g sugar
10g hazelnuts

Method

For The Panna Cotta

Heat cream, milk, vanilla and sugar and leave to infuse.

Place gelatine in cold water to soften. Dissolve softened gelatine in a little of the vanilla cream then incorporate into the remaining cream.

Pour mixture into 10cm moulds and allow to set in the fridge, ideally overnight.

Do not boil the cream for the panna cotta as this will affect the colour and make them set firmer.

> **Chef's Tip**
> Dip the panna cotta mould into very hot water for three to four seconds then tease them out of the mould for serving.

For The Strawberries

Cut strawberries into quarters, toss with a little icing sugar and leave for two hours.

For The Raspberry Sorbet

Put sugar, water, raspberries and lemon juice into a pan and simmer. Taste and adjust the acidity and sweetness, if necessary. Now blend, pass through a fine sieve and place in a shallow container in the freezer. Stir every 20 minutes until frozen and smooth.

For The Praline

Roast hazelnuts at 180°C for six minutes then rub in a cloth to remove the skins.

Place sugar in a heavy-based pan on a low heat and leave to turn into caramel. Do not stir.

Add the almonds and turn out onto very lightly oiled greaseproof paper and allow to cool.

Place the praline mix into a food processor and blend until fine crumbs are achieved. Sieve the crumbs keeping bits that don't pass through the sieve for your garnish.

Sprinkle the fine crumbs onto baking parchment and bake in low oven for one minute to allow the praline to melt, then allow to cool again and set. Use a cookie cutter to achieve circular discs.

To Serve

Place each element in a line on a rectangular plate, or slate. Place the discs on the top of each scoop of raspberry sorbet. Trail lines of praline along the outside of the plate.

120
THE LION
BAR, RESTAURANT & ROOMS

High Street, Leintwardine, Shropshire, SY7 0JZ

01547 540 203
www.thelionleintwardine.co.uk

Situated just nine miles from the culinary town of Ludlow is the picturesque village of Leintwardine, on the Shropshire and Herefordshire border. Surrounded by breathtaking views of the Welsh Marches, The Lion sits proudly beside the banks of the River Teme.

The building is believed to date back to the 1700's, when it is thought to have been a malt-house, but records show that in the 1800's it was significantly changed and converted to an Inn. In recent years The Lion fell into disrepair, suffered from flooding and eventually closed and lay empty for over a year. The present owners have extensively refurbished it while carefully retaining its original features and today it offers a warm, welcoming and stylish bar, restaurant and rooms which blend contemporary style with traditional character.

The eight en-suite bedrooms are all individually designed. The mix of modern and antique furniture and spacious modern bathrooms are a tranquil retreat for overnight guests.

Just five months after reopening, The Lion won five stars highly commended from both the AA and English Tourist Board. Diners can enjoy The Lion's award-winning food served in both the lounge and restaurant and in summer months on the terrace in the stunning south facing gardens where the lawns slope down to the gentle water of the river.

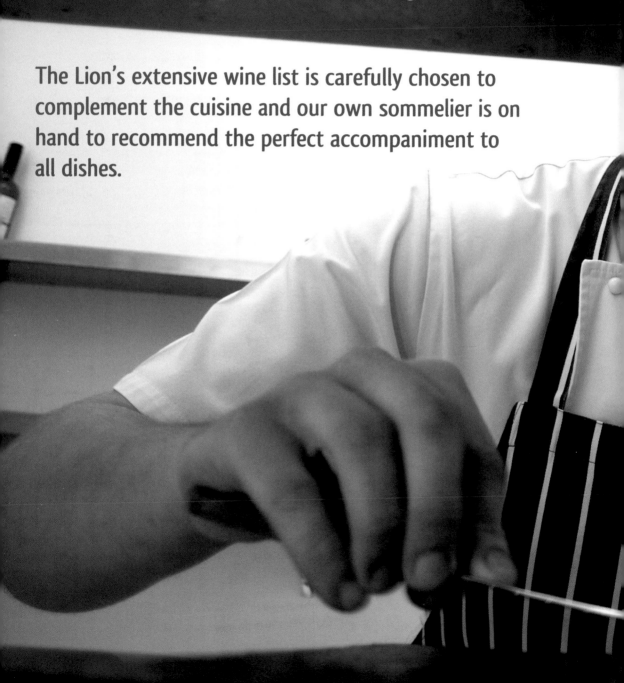

Award-winning Head Chef, Jason Hodnett was appointed to lead the kitchen team when The Lion opened in October 2010. His passion for fine food is reflected in seasonal menus that are created using the best locally sourced produce, a modern take on British food which has won him well deserved praise from both critics and the most discerning of patrons.

The Lion's extensive wine list is carefully chosen to complement the cuisine and our own sommelier is on hand to recommend the perfect accompaniment to all dishes.

POACHED WILD RAINBOW TROUT, CRAB MAYONNAISE, CELERY SALT SCONES

SERVES 4

*The Money Spider Roussane d'Arenberg 2009
(Australia)*

Ingredients

For The Rainbow Trout

1 wild rainbow trout fillet
1 sprig rosemary
1 sprig thyme
1 clove garlic
$^1/_2$ lemon
salt and pepper
50ml fish stock

Crab Mayonnaise

2 crabs
$^1/_2$ lemon
20g chives (chopped)
20g chervil (chopped)
1 egg yolk
5g white wine vinegar
50ml rapeseed oil

Scones

100g self raising flour
20g salted butter
20g parmesan cheese
3g paprika
3g celery salt
50ml milk
5g sea salt

Method

To Prepare The Trout

Lay the fillet on a sheet of greaseproof paper in an ovenproof dish, slice the garlic and remove the rosemary and thyme leaves from the stalks. Slice the lemon and place on top of the trout. Pour over the fish stock and cover with greaseproof paper. Preheat oven to 200°C and poach in the oven for four minutes. When cooked, leave to cool and then gently remove the herbs and lemon. Flip the fillet over and gently remove the skin. Tear into large flakes and season to taste.

For The Crab

Boil the crabs for eight to ten minutes depending on size, then remove and plunge into iced water to refresh. Remove the claws and, using the back of a knife, carefully crack the claws to remove the white meat. Crack the shell and remove the dead man's fingers to remove the brown meat. Mix both types in a large mixing bowl along with the diced chives, chervil, zest and juice of the lemon.

For The Mayonnaise

Blend the egg yolk with lightly warmed white wine vinegar in a food processor. Whilst continuously blitzing, very slowly drizzle in the oil until the mixture becomes thick and creamy. Add one tablespoon of hot water to adjust consistency.

Combine the crab mixture with the mayonnaise, season to taste and refrigerate until needed. Remove from the fridge for ten to 12 minutes before serving to allow the crab mayonnaise to come to temperature.

For The Scones

In a large, stainless steel bowl mix the flour, paprika, celery salt and sea salt together. Add the cold butter and rub together to make fine crumbs. Add the finely grated parmesan and mix well. Now slowly incorporate the milk to form firm dough. Rest for ten to 15 minutes then roll the dough out to quarter inch thickness between two sheets of greaseproof paper. Cut into the desired shape, brush with milk and bake for eight to ten minutes at 200°C.

To Serve

Place the crab mayonnaise in the bottom of a polished clear glass, place flaked sea trout on top, garnish with baby herbs and serve with warm scones.

12 HOUR BELLY OF PURE WELSH PORK, BUTTERNUT, LEEKS & POTATOES, BABY MUSHROOMS & RAISIN JUS

SERVES 4

Peter Mertes Pfalz Riesling 2009, Mosel
(Germany)

Ingredients

For The Pork And Jus

750g best pork belly (skin on, rib bones removed)
2 pints chicken stock
1 pint sweet cider
2 celery stalks
2 carrots
1 onion
50g each flamed and golden raisins
2 sprigs each rosemary, thyme and sage

For The Leek And Potatoes

1 leek
3 large potatoes
1 egg
2 chicken fillets
50ml double cream
40g White Beach or Shimeji mushrooms

Vegetables

1 butternut squash
1 bunch asparagus

To Garnish

crispy pig's rind

Method

To Braise The Belly Pork

Dice half the carrot, half the celery and half of the onion and garlic and place in a large ovenproof dish. Dice half of the herbs and rub into the underside of the pork belly. Place the pork belly on top of the root vegetables and pour over the cider and chicken stock. Cover with greaseproof paper and tin foil and place in a preheated oven at 120°C for 12 hours. Once cooked, remove from the tray and cool for two hours then portion into equal squares.

For The Jus

Skim off any cooking juices. Put the cooking juices into a heavy bottomed saucepan and bring to a boil. Simmer for 30 to 40 minutes until the liquid has reduced by half. Dice the remaining vegetables and fry until golden. Add the red wine and reduce by half. Now add the cooking *liquor* and bring to a gentle simmer. Strain into a clean saucepan and add the raisins and simmer for a further 15 minutes.

For The Leek And Potatoes

Blitz the chicken fillets and leek tops in a food processor then add cream, a whole egg and season. Peel potatoes and, using a small Parisienne scoop, take 30 balls from one potato and lightly fry in a little butter along with the baby mushrooms until golden. Top and tail the remaining potatoes then halve them. Using an apple corer, make a hollow in each half approximately two thirds of the potato deep. Stuff with the chicken and leek mousse and bake on greaseproof paper for 35 minutes until golden.

For The Vegetables

Peel the butternut squash and cut into one quarter inch dice. Boil in salted water for 20 minutes until soft. Blitz, pass through a fine sieve and season, adding a little butter. Blanch asparagus tips in boiling salted water for 45 seconds.

To Serve

Panfry the pork belly portions skin side down for 15 to 20 minutes until the skin is golden and crisp. Warm the butternut purée and place two to three tablespoons on the plate. Position the stuffed potato in the middle with the crispy pork belly on top. Arrange the asparagus and the Parisienne potatoes with baby mushrooms around the purée. Drizzle with a little of the raisin *jus* and serve with crispy pig's rind.

RUM & RAISIN CHEESECAKE, SPICED RAISIN PUREE, BITTER CHOCOLATE

SERVES 4

🍷 *Graham Beck Rhona Muscadel 2008
(South Africa)*

Ingredients

1 shot dark rum
33g caster sugar
100ml water
66g flamed raisins
66g golden raisins
$1/3$ tsp nutmeg
$1/6$ tsp ground cinnamon
pinch ground vanilla
60g icing sugar
200g soft cheese
50g mascarpone cheese
$1/4$ pint double cream

For The Base

175g plain flour
$1/2$ tsp bicarbonate of soda
1 tsp ground ginger
$1/2$ tsp ground cinnamon
60g butter
85g soft brown sugar
1 free range egg
4 tbsp golden syrup

Ganache

100g 70% dark chocolate
100ml double cream
50g butter

Method

For The Mix

Place both types of raisins into a heavy bottomed pan along with the caster sugar, dark rum, nutmeg, cinnamon and water. Bring to a gentle simmer and cook for 15 minutes until half of the cooking *liquor* has reduced. Remove from the heat and cool.

In a large mixing bowl, beat together the soft cheese, mascarpone and vanilla, adding the icing sugar in quarterly stages. In a separate bowl whisk the double cream to very soft peaks, add half of the cream to the soft cheese mix, fold, then add the remaining half ensuring there are no separations between the cheese mix and the cream.

For The Raisin Purée

Once the raisins have cooled, strain off the remaining fluid, retaining the liquor for the purée. In a food processor blitz half of the raisins along with half of the cooking liquor until smooth. Pass through a fine mesh sieve. Chill until needed. Retain a few raisins for garnishing and, once cooled, fold the remaining raisins into the cheesecake mix.

To Make The Ganache

Place the chocolate, butter and cream into a metal bowl over a pan of boiling water for eight to ten minutes until the chocolate and butter has melted. Pour into a plastic container and refrigerate for two to three hours.

For The Base

For the cheesecake base, sift together the flour, bicarbonate of soda, ginger and cinnamon and mix in a food processor. Add the butter and blend until the mixture resembles breadcrumbs. Stir in the sugar. Lightly beat the egg and golden syrup together then add to the food processor and pulse until the mixture clumps together. Tip the dough out, knead briefly until smooth, wrap in clingfilm and leave to chill in the fridge for 15 minutes. Preheat the oven to 180°C/Gas 4. Line two baking trays with greaseproof paper. Roll the dough out to quarter inch thickness, cut into disks and bake for 12 to 15 minutes. Cool on a wire rack and blitz to a fine crumb in a food processor. Store in an airtight container.

To Serve

Place two tablespoons of biscuit crumbs in the middle of a large slate and with a warm scoop serve the cheesecake mix on top. Take a smaller scoop of the ganache and blow torch to a fine shine. Garnish with purée and reserved raisins.

130
NUTHURST GRANGE
COUNTRY HOUSE HOTEL & RESTAURANT

Nuthurst Lane, Hockley Heath, Warwickshire, B94 5NL

01564 783 972
www.nuthurst-grange.co.uk

A stunning avenue is the approach to Nuthurst Grange Country House Hotel and Restaurant, nestled in more than seven acres of private woodlands, well-tended gardens and mature grounds with views over rolling countryside. It is a perfect luxury retreat situated in the glorious county of Warwickshire. Privately owned by Paul Hopwood, this three AA Red Star rated hotel has 19 individually decorated bedrooms to offer considerable luxury and comfort. The public areas include restful lounges, meeting rooms, a recently added modern orangery with the more traditional restaurant at its heart, offering several dining options from a simple lounge menu to its seven course tasting menu.

Our conference facilities are the perfect place to get business done with none of the usual diversions and distractions. Whether it's a day conference for five people or a corporate three day event we can make sure everything runs smoothly. Our most recent addition saw the restoration of the Stable Barn Suite, in July 2011 - a beautiful self-contained building set within the grounds of the hotel that adds to our conference facilities. It has also aided Nuthurst Grange to continue to be one of the first choice wedding venues in Warwickshire and the Midlands.

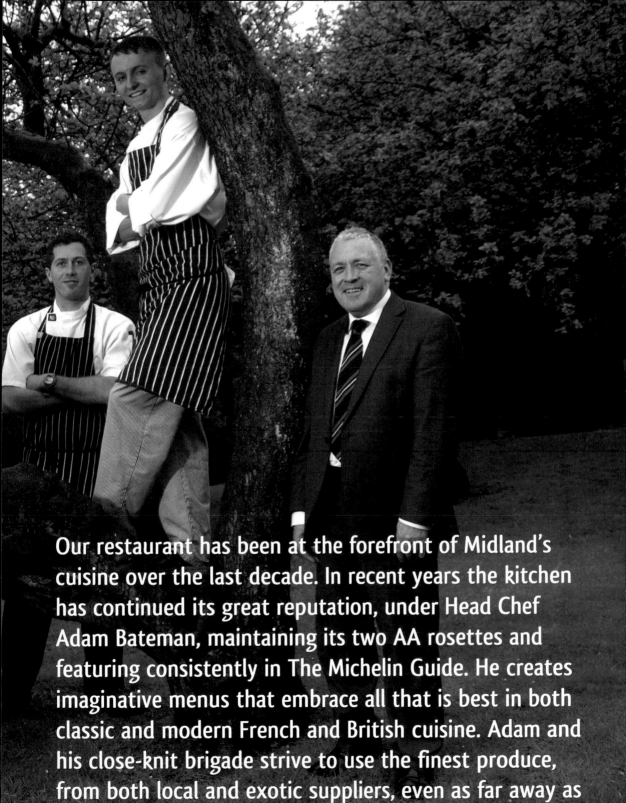

Our restaurant has been at the forefront of Midland's cuisine over the last decade. In recent years the kitchen has continued its great reputation, under Head Chef Adam Bateman, maintaining its two AA rosettes and featuring consistently in The Michelin Guide. He creates imaginative menus that embrace all that is best in both classic and modern French and British cuisine. Adam and his close-knit brigade strive to use the finest produce, from both local and exotic suppliers, even as far away as our walled gardens and grounds.

NUTHURST RABBIT, JELLY, SWEETCORN MOUSSE, CRISPY ROCKET

SERVES 4

🍷 *Oaked White Chardonnay - Cloudy Bay 2011*
(New Zealand)

Ingredients

For The Rabbit

1 rabbit (from our gardens, or local butcher)
1 stick celery
1 carrot
1 leek
2 litres water (for rabbit stock)
7 gelatine leaves (to use for jelly)

Rabbit Mousse

150ml double cream
1 slice white bread (remove crusts)
salt and pepper

For The Ballotine

5 wild garlic leaves
5 thin pancetta slices

Sweetcorn Mousse

600g sweetcorn (frozen)
200ml chicken stock
50g butter
150ml double cream

rocket leaves

Method

For The Rabbit

De-bone the rabbit, reserving the leg and loin meat, dice the carrot, celery and leek. Roast the vegetables with the rabbit bones at 180°C until dark brown. Place in a medium saucepan; add water, simmer for four hours to produce one litre of strong rabbit stock. Reserve some stock for the jelly.

For The Jelly

Soften gelatine in cold water and add to the passed rabbit stock, set as thin sheets then refrigerate.

For The Rabbit Mousse

Dice the leg meat and place in a food processor. Add the diced slice of bread and blend until smooth. Remove and fold in 150ml double cream, season with salt and pepper. Put into a piping bag.

For The Ballotine

On a sheet of clingfilm, place the pancetta into strips, place the rabbit loin on top, with the wild garlic leaves laid on top of the loin. Pipe rabbit mousse next to loin. Roll the rabbit into a ballotine or sausage shape. Poach in a water bath at 63°C for 45 minutes. After poaching chill and reserve.

For The Sweetcorn Mousse

Bring the sweetcorn, chicken stock and butter to the boil. Season then blend into a smooth purée, then chill the purée. Semi whip 150ml cream and fold in 200ml of sweetcorn purée to finish the sweetcorn mousse. Reserve.

For The Crispy Rocket

Deep fry at 170°C until the rocket stops bubbling, remove from the fryer and drain on a piece of paper towel.

To Serve

Assemble as in picture.

> **Chef's Tip**
> This dish is great for a dinner party as it can be prepared well in advance.

CONFIT SHANK, ROAST LOIN & BREAST OF LIGHTHORNE LAMB

SERVES 4

 Burgundy Givrey Chambertin 2005 (France)

Ingredients

Prepare The Day Before

1 lamb shank
1 lamb breast
1 litre chicken stock
1 small tin chopped tomatoes
2 cloves garlic
1 sprig rosemary
1tbsp capers

On The Day

1 lamb loin

Carrot Purée

2 carrots (peeled and grated)
200ml fresh orange juice

For The Lamb

8 spring onions
8 wild garlic leaves
1 packet panko breadcrumbs
2 beaten eggs
plain flour (to dust)
1 sprig rosemary
1 knob of butter

To Garnish

50g green pitted olives

Method

Day Prior To Serving: For The Shank And Breast

Place the shank and breast in a deep saucepan or ovenware dish with a lid, cover the meat with chicken stock, chopped tomatoes, garlic cloves and one sprig of rosemary. Put the lid on and place into the oven to braise at 140°C for three to four hours until meat is tender. Once the meat is tender, remove from cooking liquor. Pass the cooking liquor through a fine sieve and slowly reduce to form the sauce.

Once the shank and breast have cooled slightly, press the breast meat between two plates or baking sheets, using greaseproof paper to stop the meat sticking. Refrigerate until needed.

Flake the shank meat off the bone and place in a bowl, add the capers and season. Spoon in a little of the cooking *liquor* and roll the mixture into four equal shaped balls. Then refrigerate until needed.

On The Day: For The Carrot Purée

Grate the carrots into a small saucepan and cover with the orange juice. Cook until very tender, place in a food processor and purée until smooth then season well.

For The Shank

Remove the lamb from the fridge; roll the shank balls into flour, then beaten eggs then finally into the panko breadcrumbs ensuring they are well coated. Shallow fry until golden brown.

For The Breast And Loin

Portion the lamb breast into four even pieces and dust with a little flour.

Panfry the lamb loin in a knob of butter and a sprig of rosemary in a medium sized pan for four minutes. After two minutes add the dusted breast meat. Once cooked allow to rest for five minutes.

Whilst the lamb is resting, sauté the spring onions and wild garlic in the same pan as the lamb.

Dice the olives for garnishing.

To Serve

Assemble as in the picture.

Chef's Tip

A great complement to lamb is salty flavours such as capers, anchovies and olives. These can be substituted according to your personal taste.

NUTHURST ORCHARD APPLES, BLACK DILL, LEMONADE SHERBET

SERVES 4

 Black Muscat, Elysium
(California)

Ingredients

Compote

8 Nuthurst apples (Bramley apples as substitute)
pinch cinnamon
150g muscavado sugar
2g agar agar
1 lemon (zested)

Fennel Wafer

150g plain flour
150g icing sugar
20g ground fennel seeds
20g butter
5ml warm water

Sherbet

120ml lemonade
1 lime (juice)
120ml milk
120ml cream
40g caster sugar
black dill from our gardens
(fennel herb as substitute)

Method

For The Apple Compote

Peel, core and dice the apples, stew down with muscavado sugar, cinnamon and lemon zest. When piping hot, add agar agar and fold in to mix well. Place mix onto a small flat baking tray and allow to set. Once set cut into 2cm x 4cm rectangles.

For The Fennel Wafer

Blend the plain flour, icing sugar, ground fennel seeds, butter and warm water into a paste. Spread as thinly as possible onto greaseproof paper on a baking tray. Bake at 150°C until the mixture is dry and light golden brown in colour.
Once removed from the oven, cut wafers (whilst still hot) into 2cm x 4cm rectangles matching the same size and shape as the apple rectangles.

For The Lemonade Sherbet

Simmer lemonade with caster sugar and lime juice until the caster sugar has dissolved. Allow to cool, then add the milk and cream. Place into an ice-cream machine and churn (as per machine instructions).
Once churned, store in freezer until needed.

To Serve

Assemble as in picture.

140
THE ORANGERY RESTAURANT
AT THE MOAT HOUSE

Lower Penkridge Road, Acton Trussell, Staffordshire, ST17 0RJ

01785 712 217
www.moathouse.co.uk

Staffordshire is a county possibly better known for its iconic yellow JCB diggers and the fantastic theme parks of Alton Towers and Drayton Manor, a county of canals and an industrial heritage epitomised by the pottery industry. Beyond this though is the rich agricultural diversity and beautiful countryside of the county and it is from this background that in 1988 that the Lewis family diversified their farming business into a village restaurant and pub.

The Moat House is the former family home, transformed in 1988 into a restaurant and pub and with plenty of hard work and dedication over the years it has evolved into the uniqueness that is The Moat House of today, with its 41 luxury bedrooms.

The 16th Century manor house is a grade two listed building; it contrasts well to the bright and airy Orangery restaurant, overlooking the Staffordshire and Worcestershire canal and the moat.

Almost everything in the kitchen is sourced from one of the companies 'Food Heroes', partnerships with local suppliers that Chris Lewis has forged over the past 20 plus years.

The Moat House has collected many awards over the years reflecting a dedication to staff training,

the team produces dishes with flair and flavour under the watchful eye of executive chef Matt Davies, coupled with a long serving front of house team offering unpretentious and friendly service.

Almost everything in the kitchen is sourced from one of the companies 'Food Heroes', partnerships with local suppliers that Chris Lewis has forged over the past 20 plus years.

RAGSTONE GOAT'S CHEESE THREE WAYS, PANNA COTTA, BONBON, FONDANT, BEETROOT CARPACCIO, CANDIED WALNUTS

SERVES 4

🍷 *White Haven Pinot Noir*
(New Zealand)

Ingredients

Panna Cotta
142ml whole milk
142ml double cream
100g goat's cheese (crumbled - easier to mix)
3 gelatine leaves

Fondant
225g double cream
120g goat's cheese (crumbled)
zest of 1 lemon

Candied Walnuts
100g walnuts
100g caster sugar

Bonbon
50g goat's cheese
1 medium egg
breadcrumbs (we use Panko crumbs, available in any good Chinese food market)
30g plain flour

Beetroot Purée And Carpaccio
2 medium beetroots
lemon juice

Garnish
chicory and pea shoots

Method

For The Panna Cotta
Warm the milk and cream in a pan. Soak the gelatine in cold water for approximately five minutes. Bring the milk and cream mixture to about 90°C then pull off the heat. Add the crumbled goat's cheese and leave the mixture for a couple of minutes to infuse. Whisk until smooth and silky. Add the soaked gelatine and pass the mixture through a fine sieve. Season and pour into your 80ml moulds. Set in the refrigerator until required.

For The Fondant
Warm the cream on the stove to approximately 90°C. Remove the pan from the heat. Add the crumbled goat's cheese then whisk until smooth and silky. Season then pass through a fine strainer. Mix in the lemon zest and set in the fridge for two to three hours.

> **Chef's Tip**
> Take the fondant out of the refrigerator for 20 minutes before serving your guests.

For The Candied Walnuts
Soak the walnuts in some warm water for approximately 30 minutes. Drain then toss them in the sugar. Bake at 180°C for ten minutes and turn frequently. Crush with knife when cooled.

For The Bonbon
Blitz the goat's cheese in a food processor. Roll into balls the size of a cherry tomato. Place into refrigerator to set.

Arrange three containers; one with beaten egg, one with seasoned flour and another with the crumbs. Take out the set goat's cheese balls. Use one hand to pass them through the egg mix, then the flour, then finally using your clean hand to roll through the crumbs. Repeat this process a second time as this double coating will prevent the bonbon from bursting.

Deep fry at 180°C then season with rock salt.

For The Beetroot Purée And Carpaccio
Wash the beetroot then simmer in seasoned hot water for two hours. Slice the cooled beetroot into thin slices and then use a cutter to get a perfect round. Purée all the trimmings in a processor with seasoning and lemon juice. Pass through a fine strainer and season.

To Serve
Arrange as in picture.

FILLET OF STAFFORDSHIRE BEEF, SLOW COOKED BLADE, HAGGIS, CABBAGE CONFIT, CARAMELISED SHALLOT PUREE, PIED BLUE MUSHROOMS, ST EMILLION SAUCE

SERVES APPROX 4

 Muga Rioja Reserva
(Spain)

Ingredients

Beef Fillet
1.5kg centre fillet of Staffordshire beef

Braised Blade
1.5kg cut blade beef
3 celery stalks, 1 large leek (chopped)
fresh thyme, 3 cloves garlic
1 bottle of red wine (reduced by half)
beef stock to cover
5g parsley, 2 shallots
100ml beef *glace* (or a good beef stock)

Cabbage Confit
200g green Savoy cabbage (finely shredded)
80g pancetta, 80g shallots (finely diced)
thyme leaves, 80ml duck fat

Haggis
150g haggis
25g shallots (finely diced)
25ml beef *glace* (or a good beef stock)
150g Panko breadcrumbs, 1 egg, 50g plain flour

Shallot Purée
200g shallots (peeled and diced)
20g butter, 20ml honey, 200ml water

St Emillion Sauce
1 bottle St Emillion wine
500ml veal *jus* (buy online or in any good supermarket)
1 carrot, 1 stick celery, 1 small leek (finely diced)
a few thyme leaves
50g hard unsalted butter

Pied Blue Mushrooms
100g pied blue mushrooms (cleaned with a towel and small brush, then trimmed)
25g butter, parsley (chopped)

Method

For The Beef Fillet
Wrap the fillet in clingfilm to shape and chill for one hour. Remove clingfilm. *Seal* fillet in a hot pan then season and cook in an oven at 190°C for 12 minutes. For medium rare, cook the fillet to a core temperature of 58°C then rest for ten minutes.

For The Braised Blade
Seal the braising beef in a hot pan and place into a casserole dish. Panfry the vegetables and add to the meat. Add the reduced wine.

Add chopped garlic, salt, and enough stock to cover the meat then cook at gas mark 3/4, 180°C, for three to four hours. When cooked shred the meat and add parsley, shallots and beef *glace*. Press the meat between two containers using silicon paper and a weight. Chill until set and cut into 3cm by 4cm portions when needed. Reheat and glaze with beef *jus* before serving.

For The Cabbage Confit
Blanch the cabbage in boiling water. Sauté the shallots and diced pancetta. Add thyme leaves. Cook the blanched cabbage in duck fat until al denté. Mix together, check seasoning and keep warm.

For The Haggis
Roll the haggis into balls a little bigger than a cherry tomato then add the red wine shallots and beef *glace*. Coat the balls using the same method as in our bonbon recipe using a double coating of flour, egg and Panko crumbs. Deep fry until golden.

For The Shallot Purée
Use a heavy duty pan to melt the butter in and then caramelise the shallots. Add water and cook until soft then purée.

For The St Emillion Sauce
Sauté the vegetables in 15g of butter. Add thyme leaves then pour in the red wine and reduce by two thirds. Add veal *jus* and reduce until it coats the back of a spoon. Season and whisk in the remainder of the butter. Pass through a fine sieve.

For Pied Blue Mushrooms
Melt butter, add mushrooms, sauté till just soft, season, add parsley.

To Serve
Assemble dish as in picture. Bon appetite!

ICED MANGO PARFAIT, PINEAPPLE POACHED IN STAR ANISE, PASSION FRUIT SORBET, COCONUT RICE, MANGO PUREE

SERVES 4

Anakenna Late Harvest Viognier, offers luscious peach notes working well with the pineapple and mango (Chile)

Ingredients

Mango Parfait

4 large egg yolks
110g caster sugar
75ml water
170ml double cream
200g mango purée

Mango Purée

5 soft mangos
100g sugar
100ml water

Coconut Rice Pudding

50g pudding rice
500ml coconut milk
200ml double cream
25g caster sugar
1 egg
100g desiccated coconut
50g flour
250g Panko crumbs

Mango Sorbet

600g mango purée
60g caster sugar
360ml water

Poached Pineapple

1 pineapple
1/2 vanilla pod
1 star anise
300g sugar
600ml water

Method

For The Mango Parfait

Dissolve the sugar in water then heat to 120°C. Whisk egg yolks in a bowl until creamy and pale then pour the cooled sugar mixture onto the eggs, mixing quickly until the mixture is thick, smooth and has increased in volume (also known as pâté à bombe). In a separate bowl combine the cream and mango purée and whisk together until the mixture is very stiff. Carefully fold the egg mixture into the stiff cream and whisk until fully combined.

Line four to six small 7cm by 3cm cylinders with silicon paper, ensuring you have at least 1cm overhang at the top. Pipe the mixture into the moulds and place in the freezer to set for six hours.

For The Mango Purée

Peel and dice the mango. Boil the sugar and water mix, in a pan and add the mango pulp. Cook until it is very soft then blitz in a processor until smooth. Pass through a fine sieve.

For The Coconut Rice Pudding

Wash the rice and place into an ovenproof dish. Warm the milk and cream together and pour over the rice. Sprinkle with the sugar and mix. Cover the dish and cook at 150°C for approximately one hour 30 minutes. Increase cooking time by another ten to 20 minutes if the rice is not soft.

Remove rice from the oven then cool. Carefully shape into balls about 3cm in diameter and set in refrigerator for six hours.

When set, coat the rice by dipping into the flour, then into the beaten egg and finally into the Panko crumbs with desiccated coconut. Roll between your hands to maximise the shape and to shake off any excess. Deep fry at 190°C.

For The Mango Sorbet

Blend the mango with the sugar and water until combined. Pass through a fine sieve then churn in an ice cream maker. Freeze until needed.

For Poached Pineapple

Peel and dice the pineapple into 2cm cubes. Add sugar, water, the star anise and the scraped vanilla from a pod then bring the syrup to the boil. Pour over the pineapple and leave the pineapple to cool and infuse.

To Serve

Take out a set parfait from its tube and place onto a plate with the diced pineapple, purée, sorbet and coconut.

150
THE ORANGERY RESTAURANT
AT LOSEHILL HOUSE HOTEL & SPA

Losehill Lane, Edale Road, Hope, Peak District, Derbyshire, S33 6AF

01433 621 219
www.losehillhouse.co.uk

We are proud to reveal the Orangery Restaurant at Losehill House Hotel And Spa, which has been privately owned and managed by Paul and Kathryn Roden and their dedicated team since 2007. To find it you will need to venture along a leafy lane and, almost by chance, you'll happen across somewhere rather special. Losehill House is the only four star hotel within the heart of The Peak District National Park. This 1914 arts and crafts gem was built as a walking retreat and has since been redeveloped as a contemporary country hotel and spa. It occupies a secluded spot on the side of Lose Hill with stunning views overlooking Win Hill.

The style of the food on offer at The Orangery Restaurant has been developed over a five year period by our head chef Darren Goodwin and his team. His creative dishes are a celebration of local produce and the skills of his team. The results are really something special. Many of our guests express genuine admiration for the quality of the preparation, flavours and presentation which together create a unique dining experience in such a wonderful setting.

We feel very strongly about the quality and provenance of the ingredients and so we source them from local Peak District businesses wherever we can.

This philosophy has gone a long way towards us being awarded the Peak District Environmental Quality Mark for our commitment to the Peak District and the environment in general.

The hotel is beautifully situated in the Peak District National Park, near to Hope, equidistant from the wonderful villages of Castleton and Edale and in the midst of some of the best walking and outdoor activity countryside in England. It is a great spot for a fantastic meal, short break or holiday, or just a relaxing escape. We aim to offer our guests a relaxing experience with quality service in an unpretentious, friendly environment.

GRILLED MACKEREL, PEA MOUSSE, SQUID INK JELLY, ASPARAGUS

SERVES 4

 Chakana Torrontes
(Argentina)

Ingredients

2 mackerel (filleted and pin bones removed)
olive oil
1 lemon

Pea Mousse

150g peas
2 tsp sugar
2 leaves gelatine (softened in cold water)
150ml double cream (whipped)
30g green sorrel

Squid Ink Jelly

100ml fish stock
a frond of dill
1 leaf gelatine (softened in cold water)
5g sachet squid ink

Garnish

12 spears asparagus
12 young, red veined sorrel leaves
12 pea shoots
small amount of quality olive oil

Method

For The Fish

Trim the fish into a rectangle and slice it in half lengthways along where the pin bones were. Place in a vacuum pouch with a little olive oil, lemon juice and a few flakes of sea salt. Seal in a vacuum packer and poach in water bath at 52°C for eight minutes.

For The Pea Mousse

Cook the peas in boiling, salted and sugared water for three minutes. Drain and reserve the cooking liquid. Plunge the peas in chilled water. Now blend the peas, the two soaked gelatine leaves and 120mm of the cooking liquid in a food processor.
Add the sorrel when it has all become fairly smooth. Check the seasoning and add more salt, sugar and lemon juice if required. Now pass the mixture through a very fine sieve and leave to cool but don't allow it to set. Whip the cream and gently fold into the cooled pea liquid, place in fridge to set for around two hours.

> **Chef's Tip**
> When seasoning the pea mixture it ought to be a little over-seasoned as you will be adding whipped cream and not re-seasoning.

For The Squid Ink Jelly

Simmer the fish stock with the dill and squid ink. Correct the seasoning and add the gelatine then pass through a sieve. Pour onto a lightly oiled, flat tray. The jelly should be quite thin. Set in the fridge on a level shelf. This should set in around 30 minutes.

For Vegetables

Prepare the asparagus by cutting the tough ends off the stalks, then trim the spears and *blanch* them in boiling water for one to two minutes, depending on the thickness of the asparagus.

To Serve

Place a rectangle of squid jelly on the plate. Add a large quenelle of pea mousse onto the jelly. Arrange the asparagus, sorrel leaves and pea shoots onto the dish. Finish the mackerel by removing from the vacuum pouch and grilling it. Allow it to cool slightly and add to the plate, then finish with a little trickle of olive oil.

ELTON ESTATE VENISON, STEAMED SUET PUDDING, BEETROOT SPELT, KALE, CHERVIL ROOT, BUTTERED KALE SAMBIRANO CHOCOLATE

SERVES 6

 Herdade Sao Miguel Ciconia Tinto (Portugal)

Ingredients

6 dariole moulds (little pudding dishes, lined with clingfilm)
6 x 150g venison fillets (fully trimmed)

Pastry

60g beef suet
120g self raising flour
1/2 tsp lemon thyme leaves
small pinch salt
splash water

Filling

300g venison haunch (diced)
50g smoked bacon (diced)
20g each onion, carrot and celery (diced)
parsley (chopped)
400ml venison stock (chicken or beef would also be fine)
1 tbsp plain flour (to add body)

1 head curly kale
100g pearled spelt
200ml beetroot juice
25g Sambirano (or other high quality dark 70% chocolate)
50 - 60g Sosa Maltosec (tapioca starch)
18 chervil roots
150ml milk
20g butter (to roast chervil in)
small pinch salt

Method

For The Filling

Brown the diced venison haunch and bacon and add the diced root vegetables. Add a tablespoon of flour, then the stock and simmer for two hours. Adjust seasoning, chill and add freshly chopped parsley.

For The Pastry

Mix the flour with the suet then add salt, thyme and water. Mix into a dough then roll it out into six circles. Line six *dariole* moulds. Fill with the casserole mix, fold over the pastry and press it with a little brushed water to seal and steam for one hour. You can do this by placing in a colander inside a large pan with a tight fitting lid. Keep topping up with water.

For The Vegetables

Peel and cook the chervil root in milk until tender. Then cool it in cold water and then roast in the oven at 180°C with a little butter and salt.

Remove the stalk from the kale, pick the leaves and cook in boiling water for one minute. Remove from the water and toss in a little butter and salt.

Toast the spelt in a dry saucepan, then add the beetroot juice and simmer for 25 minutes until tender.

For The Venison

Season the fillets of venison with salt and pepper and *seal* in a frying pan. Roast in oven for four to five minutes then finish with a little butter. Leave to rest for five minutes.

> **Chef's Tip**
>
> The venison can be seasoned with ground dried cep powder, sealed in a vacuum pouch and cooked sous vide at 52°C for 12 minutes prior to browning in a pan removing the need for the roasting.

For The Chocolate Powder

Melt the chocolate in a glass or metal bowl over simmering water. Stir in 50 to 60g tapioca starch until a powder is achieved.

To Serve

Assemble as in the picture. Sprinkle the chocolate powder over the dish as a seasoning.

HONEY & ORANGE CAKE, CHOCOLATE, BLOOD ORANGE HONEYCOMB & ICE CREAM

SERVES 6

 Muscat de Rivesaltes, Chateau Cap de Fouste (France)

Ingredients

Cake
6 mini loaf tins (7 x 3cm)
70g butter
40g brown sugar
70g heather honey
1 egg
8g almonds (ground)
zest of 1 orange

Blood Orange Bubble
225g blood orange juice
50g sugar syrup
7g calcium lactate
2g xanthan gum

Alginate Bath
500ml warm water (60°C)
2.5g sodium alginate

Honeycomb
175g caster sugar
1 tbsp glucose
50ml blossom honey
50ml water
3/4 tsp bicarbonate of soda

Honey And Yoghurt Ice Cream
25g honey
65ml milk
25g crème fraiche
25g sugar
3 egg yolks
115g plain yoghurt

Chocolate Ganache
100g dark chocolate (broken into small pieces)
10g honey
10g butter
80ml double cream

Method

For The Cake
Melt the butter, honey and sugar. Fold in the flour and beat in the egg. Bake in six mini loaf tins at 170°C for 12 minutes.

For The Bubble
Thoroughly blend the ingredients, and then freeze in hemispherical ice cube tray. Then make an *alginate bath* by thoroughly blending the water and sodium alginate and heating to approximately 60°C and pour into a casserole dish.

Carefully drop the frozen blood orange into the bath, keeping the balls separate. Leave in for three minutes then remove and rinse in a bowl of fresh water.

For The Honeycomb
Heat the sugar, honey, water and glucose in a large pan until it reaches 160°C. Remove from the heat then very carefully add the bicarbonate and stir it in quickly. The mix should now rise rapidly. Tip out onto a greased baking sheet. Allow to cool and break into small pieces.

For The Ice Cream
Heat the milk and crème fraiche, beat the eggs and sugar and honey until pale, pour the warm milk over the egg mix, and cook in a pan until 80°C. Whisk in the yoghurt, chill and churn in ice cream machine.

For The Ganache
Place the chocolate pieces, honey and butter in to a bowl and melt over a pan of simmering water. Heat the cream until it simmers and then pour this over the melted chocolate mixture and stir in until smooth. Leave to cool at room temperature.

To Serve
Place warm cake, honeycomb and a quenelle of chocolate ganache. Brush melted chocolate on plate and add a scoop of ice cream.

Chef's Tip
Brush the cake with warm syrup made from orange juice and sugar for a sticky, soft glaze.

To source the xanthan gum, sodium alginate and calcium lactate use online shops such as The Home Chocolate factory, and Infusions For Chefs.

160
ORLES BARN

Wilton, Ross-on-Wye, Herefordshire, HR9 6AE

01989 562 155
www.orles-barn.co.uk

Orles Barn has origins dating back to the 14th Century and it carries on its strong ties with Herefordshire by encompassing the artisan farmers, butchers and growers in the local area as well as fish from the Gower coast. Sourcing from surrounding suppliers ensures freshness, skill and ultimately taste are at the forefront of every meal.

Located over the bridge from the market town of Ross-on-Wye, Orles Barn is a fantastic base from which to explore the area and soak up all the history, culture and activities in the Midlands and South Wales, with the assurance of a luxurious, relaxing and above all outstanding culinary experience to follow.

Dan Wall, chef director at Orles Barn took over the reins to the kitchen in 2010 and since then he has taken the local area by storm achieving 'Best Restaurant in Herefordshire' in his first year and receiving wide spread acclaim from critics and journalists ever since.

Orles Barn is the perfect place for a luxurious, relaxing and romantic break and in the summer months the large, south facing garden is ideal for lazy lunches, pre-dinner drinks and generally soaking up the sun. There are six well appointed bedrooms and suites each individually interior designed.

Herefordshire has not only been home for the three of us for most of our lives but it is also home to talented farmers, growers and butchers who supply us with local, seasonal produce which we serve throughout the year. With our roots firmly planted in the area, we have known many of our suppliers since school which gives us an amazing relationship on which to design creative, delicious dishes and produce a menu which captures the local specialties.

WOOD PIGEON & WALNUT TART, COBREY FARM ASPARAGUS

SERVES 4

🍷 *2009 Cotes du Rhone Domaine Lafond Roc-Epine or 2007 Chateauneuf du Pape Les Galets Roules (France)*

Ingredients

8 pigeon breasts
3 bunches asparagus
100g ready made puff pastry (room temperature)
100g rocket leaves
75g butter

Walnut Pesto

500g walnut halves
1 clove garlic
150g parmesan
200ml rape seed oil
salt to taste

Method

For The Walnut Pesto

Add all ingredients, except salt, together into a food processor. Blitz until almost smooth, taste and add salt if needed. Will keep in the fridge for up to six weeks.

For The Pastry

Roll the pastry out thinly and spread three teaspoons of the pesto on evenly, cook at 175°C for approximately 20 minutes or until crisp. Once cooked, trim the edges and using a sharp knife or pastry cutter to cut into even sized shapes and cool.

Blanch two thirds of the asparagus and refresh in cold water. Peel or very finely slice the remaining asparagus.

For The Pigeon

In a hot pan, cook the seasoned breasts for one minute on the skin side, turn over, add the butter and remove from the heat, rest for two minutes (for medium) and remove from the pan.

To Serve

Gently reheat the tartlets in the oven, heat the asparagus spears and strips in the warm butter. Slice the breasts in half and serve on to a warm plate.

SEARED GURNARD, CRAB CROQUETTES, BRAISED LEEKS, SAFFRON & TARRAGON SAUCE

SERVES 4

🍷 *2010 Sancerre La Clochette
or 2009 Chablis Domaine Billaud Simon
(France)*

Method

For The Crab Croquettes

Mix the cold mash with 300g of the crab meat. Season and shape this into 12 cylindrical pieces. Roll these in the flour then in beaten egg and milk and then finally cover in breadcrumbs. Chill in the fridge. Deep fry until golden, just before serving.

For The Braised Leeks

Thinly slice and wash the leeks and add them to a pan with the vegetable stock. Cook gently until soft.

For The Sauce

Combine the crab stock with the cream and bring to a boil. Then reduce the heat, add the saffron and simmer for three minutes. Add the tarragon and check the seasoning just before serving.

For The Fish

Cut each Gurnard fillet into three even pieces, giving 12 pieces, three per portion. Season the flesh side and place the fillets into a semi-hot pan, skin side down, and cook gently for about three minutes or until the skin crisps. Unless you have a pan big enough, use two pans as this will keep the heat and ensure the skin crisps up. Turn the fillets over and remove from the heat. Leave to rest for two minutes in the pan.

To Serve

Assemble as in picture.

Ingredients

4 large Gurnard (filleted)
400g white crab meat
400g potato (mashed and chilled)
50g flour
1 egg and 150ml milk (beaten together)
100g breadcrumbs
250g leeks
200ml double cream
100ml crab or shellfish stock
100ml vegetable stock
2 pinches saffron
25g tarragon

DARK CHOCOLATE & BANANA FONDANT, BANANA MILKSHAKE, CARAMELISED BANANA & CHOCOLATE ICE CREAM

SERVES 6

 2006 Chateau Loupiac Gaudiet
(France)

Ingredients

Fondants

100g dark chocolate (buttons or chopped)
10g plain flour
2 eggs
2 egg yolks
100g butter
55g caster sugar
6 x 6cm rings
25g butter and 20g dark cocoa (to line the rings)

Milkshake

3 ripe bananas (almost black is a good thing!)
150ml double cream
100g vanilla ice cream

Garnish

2 ripe bananas
6 balls chocolate ice cream
75g caster sugar (to caramelise the banana slices)

Method

For The Fondants

Melt the 100g of butter and the chopped chocolate in a *bain-marie* bowl over simmering water then leave to cool slightly. Beat the eggs and yolks with the sugar and flour. Mix the two mixtures together thoroughly. Pour into rings or moulds that have been coated with butter and cocoa powder. Chill for one hour until set.

Chef's Tip

Putting a layer of sliced banana in the middle of the chocolate mixture makes a great addition. But try and use really ripe bananas.

For The Banana Milkshake

In a food blender, mix three of the bananas, the vanilla ice cream and cream and blend until smooth.

For The Caramelised Banana

Slice the remaining bananas and arrange the slices into six portions, sprinkle on the remaining sugar. On a tray, either under a hot grill or carefully with a blow torch, caramelise the slices, then transfer to a plate.

To Serve

Bake the fondants in the oven at 180°C for about 11 minutes, they should just wobble when taken out. Rest for a minute then turn out onto a plate.

Serve with the chocolate ice cream and caramelised banana and the milk shake in a glass.

170
PEEL'S RESTAURANT
BY MARTYN PEARN

Shadowbrook Lane, Hampton-in-Arden, Solihull, B92 0EN

01675 446 080
www.peelsrestaurant.co.uk

Set in the historic courtyard of Hampton Manor, the former home of Sir Frederick Peel, son of Prime Minister Sir Robert Peel, Peel's Restaurant provides an experience that is rich in history and yet is sophisticatedly modern.
Our philosophy is that fine dining is about food and not formality, and that it should be affordable too.

Executive Head Chef Martyn Pearn draws on a classical background that has seen him hold a Michelin star at La Reserve in Bordeaux France and at Buckland Manor in Worcestershire for a period of over 12 years. Today Martyn's cooking has an honesty and restraint that is refreshingly unfussy and consistently demonstrates his craft by delivering perfectly cooked, modern British food with bold and gutsy flavours.

Martyn sources produce with quality and consistency as his guiding principles and the menus are changing continually to reflect this. Warwickshire and the surrounding counties provide inspiration to source local produce where possible.

Within Hampton Manor, plans to restore the estate's walled garden to grow fresh produce are being shaped by Martyn and his team.

Hampton Manor is privately owned and has been beautifully restored. Set in 45 acres of parkland, the house is approached by a sweeping tree-lined drive and has traditional charm combined with contemporary chic. It offers 15 luxurious, individually designed bedrooms that have been created for comfort, pleasure and indulgent escapism.

Peel's Restaurant by Martyn Pearn: an award winning chef, a commitment to exceptional service, an unrivalled setting, the ingredients of an unforgettable experience.

Martyn Pearn's cooking has an honesty and restraint that is refreshingly unfussy and consistently demonstrates his craft by delivering perfectly cooked, modern British food with bold and gutsy flavours.

VALE ASPARAGUS

SERVES 4

 Entre-Deux-Mers 2010 Chateau Turcaud
Vignoble Maurice Robert Bordeaux (France)

Ingredients

20 jumbo asparagus tips
salt and pepper
60g tempura flour
1 bottle chilled sparkling water
100g baby leaf spinach
300ml double cream
200ml mayonnaise
50ml white truffle oil
1 punnet pea shoots

Method

Peel the asparagus 3cm from the tips down to the base, keeping the green part of the peelings.

In a pan of boiling, salted water *blanch* 12 peeled asparagus so that they still have a slight crunch. Refresh in cold water and drain well. Cut the remaining eight in half on a slight angle and reserve for the tempura.

Take the thickest eight of the 12 blanched tips and cut to approximately 5cm lengths, keeping the trimmings for the velouté.

> **Chef's Tip**
>
> Only use Vale of Evesham asparagus as it's the best in the world.

For The Velouté

In a high-speed blender, blitz the remaining four blanched asparagus spears along with the cooked trimmings and blanched spinach until smooth and bright green. Then pass through a fine sieve and add the mayonnaise and cream. Season and leave to chill in the fridge.

For The Tempura

Mix the tempura flour and water until it forms a light batter. Keep chilled in the fridge.

To Serve

With a Japanese mandolin, slice the remaining spears lengthways and arrange equally between four serving plates.

Warm a deep pan of sunflower oil to approximately 160°C and deep fry the remaining 16 halves of asparagus in the batter and fry until crisp and golden. Remove, drain and arrange equally on top of the sliced asparagus.

Lightly drizzle with truffle oil and serve the chilled velouté, garnish with pea shoots.

CANON OF NEW SEASONS LAMB, SMOKED KING EDWARDS MASH, WHITE ONION & ANCHOVY PUREE & GARLIC NUGGETS

SERVES 4

Shiraz 'The Freedom 1843' 2006
Langmeil Winery Barossa Valley (Australia)

Ingredients

2 canons of lamb (from the best end)

Mash

3 large King Edwards potatoes (peeled)
50g smoked butter
500ml double cream
salt and pepper
30g oak smoking chips

Onion Purée

2 white onions (peeled and chopped)
1 garlic clove (crushed)
salt and pepper
100ml olive oil
2 anchovy fillets
2 sprigs thyme
100ml double cream

Garlic Nuggets

250ml milk
20g butter
20g plain flour
4 garlic cloves (crushed)
10g mature cheddar cheese (grated)
salt and pepper
pinch of nutmeg
flour, egg and breadcrumbs

Method

For The Nuggets

In a heavy-bottomed pan, melt the butter slowly over a low heat. Add the flour and stir well to make a *roux*. Meanwhile, warm the milk, garlic and nutmeg then strain through a fine sieve onto the *roux* and mix well. Season and add the cheese.

Turn out onto a greased tray and refrigerate until set.

Cut out into nuggets and coat with the flour, egg and bread crumbs. Reserve until needed.

Deep fry the nuggets just before serving.

For The Mash

Spread the smoking chips over a shallow roasting tray and place the cream in a high sided bowl in the centre of the tray. Cover the whole thing with tin foil and cook in a preheated oven for 40 minutes at 160°C.

Cook and mash the potatoes in the usual way, add the smoked butter and cream to your liking and season.

Keep warm until needed.

> **Chef's Tip**
> King Edwards' make the best mash.

For The Onion Purée

In a heavy-bottomed pan, cook the onion without it colouring, along with the garlic and thyme in olive oil for 20 minutes. Then add the anchovy and cook for a further 20 minutes with the lid on the pan until soft.

Blitz in a blender until smooth, adding the cream to enrich it and to give a velvety consistency. Keep warm until needed.

For The Lamb

Cook the lamb to your liking and leave to rest in a warm place. If you like your lamb cooked medium then place in oven at 180°C for 12 minutes.

To Serve

Make a drag with a spoon of onion purée across four flat serving plates, pipe a swirl of smoked mash, slice the lamb and arrange over the four plates, dot the deep fried nuggets around, garnish with some fine beans and carrots. Sauce with a little lamb *jus*.

KAFFIR LIME LEAF PANNA COTTA WITH MANGO SOUP, MACERATED MANGO & BLACK PEPPER SHORTBREAD

SERVES 4

Montlouis - Sur-Loire Moelleux 'Romulus' 2009
Domaine de la Taille aux Loups - Jacky Blot
Loire Valley (France)

Ingredients

Panna Cotta

175ml whole milk
125ml double cream
50g sugar
3g gelatine
3 kaffir lime leaves

Mango Soup

1 mango (peeled and roughly chopped)
100ml water
100g fructose sugar
pinch dried chilli

Macerated Mango

1/2 mango
1 tsp fructose sugar
1/4 small chilli (very finely chopped)

Black Pepper Shortbread

87.5g plain flour
1/4 tsp baking powder
1/4 tsp Maldon sea salt
1/2 tsp crushed black peppercorns
55g cold, unsalted butter (cubed)
50g caster sugar
1 egg yolk
17.5ml olive oil
extra caster sugar for dusting

Garnish

coriander cress

Chef's Tip

The salt in the shortbread and soup encourages sweetness, only use Maldon sea salt flakes.

Method

For The Shortbread

Preheat oven to 150°C. Sift the flour and baking powder into a bowl and then add the salt and black pepper.

Cream together the butter and sugar then add the mix of dry ingredients until it resembles breadcrumbs.

Combine the egg yolk and olive oil and gradually add to the mix, turning when the dough comes together. Place in the fridge to rest for 20 minutes.

When rested, roll out between two sheets of parchment to about 5mm thick and put back in the fridge for ten minutes on a baking sheet. Remove from the fridge and carefully peel off the top sheet of parchment and bake in the preheated oven for 14 to 18 minutes.

Remove from the oven and, whilst still warm, cut into the desired shape and dust with caster sugar and cool on a wire rack.

For The Panna Cotta

Crush the kaffir lime leaves and place in a pan with the milk and warm it slightly (but do not boil). Set aside to infuse for ten minutes.

Add the cream and sugar to the pan and warm gently. Soak the gelatine in ice cold water until soft. When the sugar has dissolved, pass through a sieve to remove the lime leaves. Add the gelatine and when it has dissolved, pass through a sieve and pour into the 75ml moulds and set in the fridge.

For The Mango Soup

Warm together the fructose sugar, water and the dried chilli until the sugar has dissolved to make sugar syrup. Pass through a sieve to remove the chilli flakes and allow to cool.

When the syrup has cooled slightly, put the mango in a blender and blend whilst gradually adding the syrup. When it is a nice pouring consistency stop adding the syrup, pass through a sieve and put in the fridge to chill.

For The Macerated Mango

Cut the mango into 3mm dice combine with the finely chopped chilli and the teaspoon of fructose sugar. Keep at room temperature to macerate until needed.

To Serve

Turn the panna cottas out of their moulds into the middle of a bowl, spoon around the macerated mango and neatly pour the soup around. Garnish with the coriander cress and serve the shortbread on the side.

180
THE RED LION

Main Street, East Haddon, Northamptonshire, NN6 8BU

01604 770 223
www.redlioneasthaddon.co.uk

The Red Lion is situated in the idyllic village of East Haddon in Northamptonshire. It is a joint venture between Nick Bonner and the Michelin-starred Chef Adam Gray.

This is by no means a quiet country restaurant and the crowds seem to be flocking to The Red Lion. As the name might suggest, it is a country pub made into a restaurant with seven stunning boutique style bedrooms. In the kitchen, Gray exercises his culinary skills to produce food which has delighted and impressed critics and customers alike, and has recently been awarded a Michelin Bib Gourmand and an entry into the Good Food Guide 2012.

The Red Lion is housed in a beautifully thatched sandstone building which oozes country pub appeal, with well-tended gardens and a large terrace eating area. Adjacent to The Red Lion is a beautifully restored barn which has been transformed into the Shires Cookery School under the guidance of The Red Lion team. It provides numerous culinary courses from bread making through to chocolate master classes.

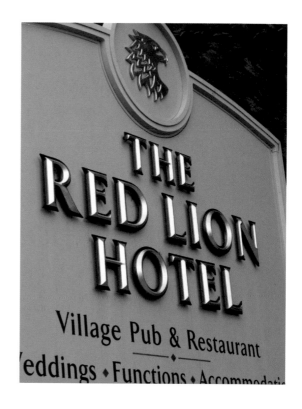

The Red Lion provides those who come from near or far with the kind of 'familiar-yet-fresh' food that Gray became known for in his various tenures elsewhere. Provenance is paid close attention to in the menus, with good use of the kind of produce you would find nearby and a close eye for seasonality. Many of the dishes on offer herald back to British classics from the last few decades that are updated for the modern crowd with classic combinations of flavour.

The aim of The Red Lion is to serve consistently good quality, simple food with friendly and attentive service in a relaxed and comfortable atmosphere.

MARINATED SALMON WITH FRESH HORSERADISH & CAPERS

SERVES 6 - 8

🍷 *Gewürtzraminer, Mission Estate, Hawke's Bay, 2009 (New Zealand)*

Method

Mix the ingredients together in a bowl to make the marinade.

Spread the marinade on the flesh side of the salmon pieces, then wrap them tightly in clingfilm.

Leave to marinade for 24 hours in the fridge.

Wash the marinade from the salmon and pat dry with a piece of kitchen towel.

To Serve

Slice the marinated salmon into $^1/_2$cm slices and arrange them neatly in a circle on the serving plate.

Mix the fine capers with the rapeseed oil and arrange evenly over the salmon.

With a micro grater, grate the raw horseradish evenly over the salmon.

Garnish with the micro coriander leaves.

Ingredients

Marinated Salmon

2kg piece fresh salmon (with skin on)
25g salt
25g sugar
5g ground white pepper
zest of $^1/_2$ lemon
$^1/_2$ bunch dill (roughly chopped)

To Garnish

100g fine capers
200g piece fresh horseradish (peeled)
micro coriander leaves
100ml Farrington's Mellow Yellow Rapeseed Oil

BRAISED RED WINE BEEF WITH SMOKED BACON CABBAGE & CREAMY MASHED POTATOES

SERVES 6

Pinot Noir, Mission Estate, Central Otago, 2007 *(New Zealand)*

Ingredients

6 x 200g beef cheeks
1 bottle red cooking wine
1 onion (peeled and quartered)
2 carrots (peeled and halved)
4 sticks celery (halved)
$^1/_2$ bulb garlic
1 leek (washed and quartered)

marinate all the above ingredients in the red wine for 24 hours

Farrington's Mellow Yellow Rapeseed Oil
(for frying)

Red Wine Beef Gravy

1 sprig thyme
2 bay leaves
3 litres chicken stock
$^1/_2$ litre veal/beef stock

Smoked Bacon Cabbage

1 small Savoy cabbage (finely shredded)
8 smoked bacon rashers (cut into 1cm strips)
75g unsalted butter
salt and pepper

Creamy Mashed Potatoes

3kg King Edward/Maris Piper potatoes (peel, chop
and boil in water until tender)
200ml semi skimmed milk
100g unsalted butter (cold and diced)
salt and pepper

Method

For The Beef

Remove all the ingredients from the red wine marinade and drain off all the wine.

Seal the marinated beef in rapeseed oil in a thick bottom frying pan until lightly coloured all over. Then remove and place in a colander to remove any excess oil.

Add all the prepared vegetables to the frying pan and colour until golden brown. Add thyme and bay leaves.

Place the sealed beef and the browned vegetables in a thick bottomed, deep saucepan and add all the red wine from the marinade. Bring to the boil to reduce the quantity of liquid by three quarters.

Cover the beef and vegetables with the chicken stock and veal/beef stock then bring it up to the boil and simmer very gently for two and a half to three hours. When the beef is very tender remove it from the cooking *liquor*.

Pass the cooking *liquor* through a fine sieve and return it to the stove. Bring the *liquor* up to the boil and reduce it until the desired consistency is required.

For The Smoked Bacon Cabbage

Heat a thick bottomed saucepan to a medium heat and add the bacon rashers. Cook the bacon rashers until they have slightly coloured, then add the butter.

When the butter starts to foam, add the shredded Savoy cabbage and a tablespoon of water. Mix the cabbage with the bacon and continue cooking for a further ten to 12 minutes on a medium heat until the cabbage is tender.

Remove the bacon and cabbage from the heat and check the seasoning with salt and pepper. Leave to drain in a colander until needed.

For The Creamy Mashed Potatoes

Put the cooked potatoes and half of the cold butter through a potato ricer and into a large saucepan. Return the saucepan to the heat and slowly incorporate the remaining butter and milk, heating gently as it is being added. Check seasoning.

To Serve

Pipe a peak of creamy mashed potato at the back of the serving plate. Place the hot smoked bacon cabbage in a disc in front of the mashed potato. Sit the braised wine beef on top of the cabbage. Pour the red wine beef gravy into a sauce jug and serve separately.

DARK CHOCOLATE CARAMEL CREAM, JAFFA ORANGE & WARM VANILLA DOUGHNUTS

SERVES 8

 Rutherglen Muscat, All Saints Estate (Australia)

Ingredients

Dark Chocolate Caramel Cream

180g caster sugar
50ml water
140g double cream
350g dark chocolate 64%
90g egg yolks
10g caster sugar
390ml whipping cream

Jaffa Orange Jelly

1 litre Tropicana orange juice
40g caster sugar
12g *orange compound*
2 1/2 leaves gelatine (soaked in cold water)

Vanilla Doughnuts

250ml milk
500g plain flour
7g fresh yeast (or 1/2 packet of dried yeast)
pinch of salt
50g caster sugar
1 egg
100g unsalted butter
1 vanilla pod (split in half and seeds scraped)

Method

For The Dark Chocolate Caramel Cream

Place the caster sugar and water into a thick-bottomed, clean, dry, stainless steel saucepan. Place on a medium heat and cook the sugar and water until it reaches a light caramel stage.

Pour in the double cream, stirring constantly. Be careful not to splash any on your hands as this will burn!

Melt the dark chocolate in a clean, dry bowl and place over a pan of boiling water. Ensure the water does not touch the bottom of the bowl. Stir the dark chocolate until it is all melted with no lumps.

Whisk together the egg yolks and sugar to a light whipped stage in a mixing machine.

Once the caramel is quite cool add it to the melted chocolate.

Fold in the whipped egg yolks and sugar.

Whip the cream to a soft peak and fold into chocolate mix.

The chocolate can now be put into a suitable container and chilled until needed. This will take a minimum of one hour.

Jaffa Orange Jelly

Reduce the one litre of Tropicana orange juice to 500ml.

Add all the other ingredients and ensure they are all dissolved before passing the mixture through a fine sieve.

Set in the desired serving glasses and chill until needed.

For Vanilla Doughnuts

Warm the milk and mix in the yeast.

Separately, mix all the dried ingredients together and place on a mixing machine then, while the machine is mixing on a low speed, add the butter in small pieces until it is fully incorporated and add the fresh vanilla seeds.

Beat the egg and pour into the mix, then finally add the milk.

Mix for about ten minutes until it becomes elasticised dough. Place the dough in a bowl, clingfilm and put in a warm place. Let the dough prove for about 25 minutes until it has doubled in size.

Lightly flour the work surface and roll out the dough to a one centimetre thickness. Cut the dough into round shapes using a doughnut cutter and rest it in the fridge for 20 minutes.

Deep fry the doughnuts at 175°C then roll in sugar and serve.

To Serve

Arrange on a plate as per the picture.

190
SEASONS RESTAURANT

Colwall Park, Colwall, Malvern, Worcestershire, WR13 6QG

01684 540 000
www.colwall.co.uk

Seasons Restaurant is located within the independently owned and run Colwall Park, a friendly, Edwardian-style hotel situated on the sunny western side of the breathtaking Malvern Hills. Built by Roland Cave Browne Cave in 1905 for the Colwall racecourse, it has been owned by Iain and Sarah Nesbitt since the year 2000. In addition to the comfort of the 22 individually decorated bedrooms, there are function facilities that can cater for eight to 80 people.

Stunning, secluded gardens have footpaths leading directly onto the Malvern Hills, where you can take delight in the spectacular views over the surrounding six counties; from the Cotswolds to the Black Mountains of Wales.

Seasons Restaurant is featured in both Michelin and The Good Food Guides and has been awarded two AA-Rosettes. They have also won the Birmingham Area Restaurant Of The Year Award.

Head Chef James Garth, who trained and worked at Paul Heathcote's of Longridge, prepares gourmet food within the contemporarily furnished, oak-panelled restaurant. Using the very best possible ingredients, locally sourced where possible, he produces the finest of modern British cuisine. Locals and residents alike can also enjoy the friendly and popular Lantern Bar which benefits from crackling log fires and an array of real ales and superb wine. The brasserie style menu offers local produce and freshly made food.

Head Chef James Garth, who trained and worked at Paul Heathcote's of Longridge, prepares gourmet food within the contemporarily furnished, oak-panelled restaurant. Using the very best possible ingredients, locally sourced where possible, he produces the finest of modern British cuisine.

HAM HOCK, LITTLE HEREFORD CHEESE & PICCALILLI TIAN WITH POTATO & GHERKIN SALAD, GRANARY TOAST & PEA SHOOTS

SERVES 8

🍷 *Terra de Lobos Castelão, Cabernet Sauvignon (Portugal)*

Ingredients

8 x 9cm metal rings or cling film lined ramekins

Tian

2 ham hocks
1 carrot (peeled and chopped)
1 onion (peeled and chopped)
2 sticks celery (chopped)
10 sprigs tarragon (picked and chopped)
120g Hereford cheese (grated)
(any other hard cheese will work as well)

Potato And Gherkin Salad

2 large potatoes (very finely diced and blanched)
4 large gherkins (very finely diced)
3 heaped tbsp mayonnaise
chives (finely chopped)
salt and pepper
mix all salad ingredients together

12 slices granary bread
pea shoots

Piccalilli

$^1/_4$ cauliflower (cut into very small florets)
1 onion and 3 shallots (very finely diced)
$^1/_4$ cucumber (very finely diced)
200ml white wine vinegar
100ml malt vinegar
$^1/_2$ small chilli
1 tsp turmeric
115g sugar
10g English mustard
1 tbsp cornflour
salt and pepper

Method

Cover the ham hocks with cold water and add the vegetables. Bring to a boil and simmer for two to three hours. Keep topping up the water so that it is above the hocks. When you can pull the bone out with ease, remove the ham from the water. When it is cold enough to handle, pick the meat from the bones and gristle. Mix a little of the ham stock with the ham and season with tarragon.

Reform the cheese into a disc by rolling the grated cheese between two pieces of greaseproof paper. Cut the disc to the same size as the mould you are using. One cheese disc per tian.

For The Tian

Half fill the mould with the ham mix. Add a cheese disc then top with another layer of ham mix. Chill in fridge.

For The Piccalilli

Place the cauliflower, onion, shallots and cucumber in a bowl and season. Bring the vinegars and chilli to a boil, then leave to cool. Mix together the turmeric, sugar, mustard and cornflour. When the vinegar mix is cool take out the chilli and add a little to the sugar mix. Then bring back to the boil.

Whisk in the sugar mixture until it has blended together and cook for two and a half minutes. Mix in the uncooked vegetables and pour into a sterilised jar then chill.

Lightly toast the bread. Remove the crusts and cut each slice into two triangles.

To Serve

Mix all the salad ingredients together and season to taste. Remove the tian from the mould and spread a thin layer of piccalilli on top. Arrange three triangles of granary toast, a spoon full of potato salad and a few pea shoots to garnish.

SEARED FILLET OF HALIBUT WITH SAFFRON TURNED POTATOES, BUTTERED SPINACH & A WHITE WINE SAUCE

SERVES 4

C J Pask Unoaked Chardonnay, Hawke's Bay
(New Zealand)

Ingredients

4 x 150g skinless halibut fillets
oil
lemon juice

White Wine Sauce

2 shallots (sliced)
1 clove garlic (chopped)
1 tbsp vegetable oil
175ml white wine
300ml fish stock
200ml double cream
salt and pepper

Saffron Potatoes

12 new potatoes
saffron

150g blanched peas
150g picked broad beans
4 tomatoes (peeled, deseeded and diced)
chives and dill (chopped)
12 broccoli florets
12 pieces baby fennel
$1/2$ bag of spinach
15g butter
1 garlic clove (peeled)

Method

For The Sauce

Sweat off the shallots and garlic in the oil without browning. Add the white wine and reduce by two thirds. Now add the fish stock and reduce by half then add the cream and simmer for three minutes. Sieve into a clean pan and set aside. Season to taste.

For The Saffron Potatoes

Trim the potatoes into barrel shapes. Cover with seasoned, boiling water and a pinch of saffron. Once nearly cooked drain the saffron liquid and leave them to cool. Reduce the saffron liquid by half.

For The Halibut

Heat up a non-stick frying pan then add a little oil. Gently add the seasoned halibut to the hot oil, service side down and cook for three minutes. Turn over the halibut and cook for another one minute according to the thickness of the fish and how you like it cooked. Season again with a little salt and squeeze of lemon juice.

For The Vegetables

Cook the baby fennel and broccoli in seasoned boiling water. Cook the spinach in a pan with the butter. Stir in the garlic with a fork.

Reheat the potatoes in the saffron liquid.

Reheat the cream sauce back and add the peas, broad beans, diced tomatoes and herbs.

To Serve

Drain the spinach and split into four bowls place the halibut on top, arrange the saffron potatoes, fennel and broccoli around the halibut, spoon over the sauce.

REFRESHING LEMON POSSET WITH RASPBERRY SAUCE, SUMMER BERRIES & SHORTBREAD BISCUITS

SERVES 8

🍷 *Gerwürztraminer, Pfaffenheim (France)*

Ingredients

Posset

850ml fresh double cream
325g sugar
3 lemons (zest and juice)

Raspberry Sauce

300g frozen raspberries
100g sugar
juice of ¹/₂ lemon

Shortbread Biscuits

125g sugar
250g butter
375g plain flour

To Serve

fresh strawberries
fresh raspberries
fresh blueberries

Method

For The Posset

Bring the cream, sugar and lemon zest to a boil. Simmer for three to four minutes then, over an ice bath, strain over the lemon juice and stir together. Set aside for 20 minutes then divide into your chosen glasses. Place in fridge to fully set.

For The Raspberry Sauce

Place raspberries in a hot, dry pan. Add the lemon juice and sugar then cook quickly. When the sauce thickens and the right consistency is reached, pass through a sieve and cool quickly.

For The Shortbread Biscuits

Combine all the ingredients together but do not overwork. Leave to rest for 20 minutes. Preheat the oven to 160°C. Roll the shortbread paste out then cut your desired shape and place onto a non stick baking tray. Bake for ten to 15 minutes until slightly browned. Remove from the oven when cooked and leave to cool, dusted with caster sugar.

To Serve

Arrange the lemon posset on the plate. Drizzle with the raspberry sauce. Decorate with shortbread biscuits and summer berries.

200
SIMPSONS
RESTAURANT WITH ROOMS

20 Highfield Road, Edgbaston, Birmingham, B15 3DU

0121 454 3434
www.simpsonsrestaurant.co.uk

Simpsons Restaurant led the way in the resurgence of Birmingham, helping the Midlands become 'the gourmet capital of the UK'*. It has been the exemplar of Midlands gastronomy, carving a path for others to follow since it first achieved its Michelin Star at its previous location in Kennilworth, Warwickshire and which it has retained since moving to leafy Edgbaston in 2004.

Under the tutelage of chef-patron Andreas Antona, the restaurant has also served as a culinary production line; setting countless chefs on their way to success.

Ferran Adria's El Bulli influenced chefs from around the world, offering them inspiration and the chance to develop levels of technical brilliance. Simpsons has done something similar on a regional scale, with its inimitable DNA on many of the region's finest chefs, including Glynn Purnell, Andy Waters, Marcus and Jason Eaves, Matt Davies, and their very own Luke Tipping. And it achieved international status when Head Chef Adam Bennett, supported by Kristian Curtis, represented the UK in the renowned Bocuse D'Or World Chef competition.

Simpsons is light and airy, with a sumptuous dining room that overlooks immaculate lawns near to Birmingham's Botanical Gardens. Classical dishes prepared under the watchful eye of his team leaders, Chef Director Luke Tipping and Head Chef Adam Bennett, scintillate the senses.

*BBC Olive Magazine 2011

Andreas believes in excellent hospitality - from the moment you arrive at the relaxed Georgian country house location, greeted by the first welcoming smile of the nurtured front of house team, you feel relaxed, in excellent company. The brigade believes in the finest ingredients, sourced from the best world suppliers, cooked simply, adhering to classic methods, rather than faddy trends.

Flavours are enhanced, never masked, simplicity is the golden rule. Simpsons eschews needless complication in favour of unfussy flavours that seduce the palate. It is truly the Midland's star act.

CITRUS CURED ORGANIC SALMON WITH AVOCADO PUREE & SEVRUGA CAVIAR

SERVES 4

 Loire Valley Sancerre Les Baronnes: Domaine Henri Bourgeois 2010 (France)

Ingredients

Salmon And Cure

300g piece of organic salmon (skinned and boned)
80g coarse salt
120g granulated sugar
6g juniper berries (chopped)
6g white peppercorns (crushed)
^{1}/2 bunch fresh dill (coarsely chopped)
1 pink grapefruit
1 orange (this includes some for the garnish)

Garnish

the reserved citrus segments
25ml water
^{1}/2 avocado
1 tsp lemon juice
salt and white pepper
small tin of Sevruga or Avruga caviar
a selection of herbs - chervil, dill and chives

Method

For The Cured Salmon

Peel the skin and pith away from the flesh of the oranges and grapefruits then cut four segments from each and reserve for the garnish. Slice the rest of the fruit thinly and reserve it. Combine the salt, sugar, spices and dill.

Lay a large sheet of clingfilm over a stainless steel or glass tray. Lay half the fruit slices on top of the clingfilm to approximate the shape of your salmon. Spread half of the salt mixture over the fruit and follow with the salmon.Top the salmon with the remaining salt followed by the rest of the citrus fruits.

Finally, wrap the salmon in the clingfilm and leave in the fridge for 18 to 24 hours. When the salmon is firm and the texture even, then it is ready.

Rinse the salmon in cold water, discard the marinade, dry the fish and wrap in fresh clingfilm. Chill for a further four to six hours before serving.

For The Garnish

Peel the avocado and cut into rough pieces. Season with salt, pepper and lemon juice. Place the avocado in the bowl of a liquidiser and add the water on a high speed to give a smooth purée.

Cut the reserved citrus segments into triangular sections and reserve.

Pick small sprigs from the chervil and dill. Cut the chives into long sections.

To Serve

Cut the salmon into slices about ^{1}/2cm thick and lay two on each plate. Season the slices with a little sea salt and pepper.

Arrange the citrus fruits, avocado, caviar and herbs along the length of the two slices and serve.

> **Chef's Tip**
> The citrus counteracts the richness of the salmon, giving a great balance with the salty caviar.

Photographs by Jodi Hinds
www.jodihinds.com/blog Twitter: @jodihinds

ROAST LOIN & SLOW-COOKED SHOULDER OF CORNISH LAMB, RADISH, FETA CHEESE, GREEN BEANS, CHICKPEAS & LOVAGE

SERVES 4

🍷 *Rhone Valley Crozes Hermitage Domaine Delas 2008 (France)*

Ingredients

Slow-cooked Lamb Shoulder

1kg piece of lamb shoulder (boned out)
2 cloves of garlic
sprig of thyme
enough duck or goose fat to cover
the lamb in a snugly-fitting pan

To Cook The Chickpeas

200g dried chickpeas
1 carrot (peeled)
$1/2$ onion (peeled)
1 stick celery
1 sprig of thyme
1 bay leaf
1 clove garlic (peeled)

For The Loin

2 loin of lamb (trimmed but with fat layer intact)
2 cloves garlic (cracked)
4 sprigs thyme
2 tbsp vegetable oil

Garnish

2 tbsp plain flour
4 slices of slow-cooked lamb shoulder
15 radishes, washed
4 tbsp cooked chickpeas
50g butter
pinch of salt and sugar
75g feta cheese (diced)
200g French beans (trimmed)
150ml basic lamb *jus*
1 tbsp chopped lovage leaves

Chef's Tip

Cook the lamb early and rest it

Method

For The Slow-cooked Lamb Shoulder

Season the lamb well with salt. Heat the fat with the garlic and thyme then add the lamb. Simmer very gently for about 20 minutes then cover the pan and cook in the oven at 90°C for around four hours or until completely tender. Remove from the oven and lift the lamb out of the fat. Pick through the meat, which should break apart easily, discarding any fat and sinew. When you have all the meat together, shred into a bowl.
Take the two cooked garlic cloves and squeeze out the purée into the lamb. Season with black pepper and salt the mix in a little of the duck fat - just enough to moisten and bind. Line a suitably sized container with clingfilm, press the mixture in and wrap well. Place in the fridge and put something heavy on top to press the mixture as it chills. Leave overnight to set.

For The Chickpeas

Soak the chickpeas overnight in double their volume of water. Drain the chickpeas and rinse in fresh water. Combine all the ingredients in a large pan and add double the volume of water to chickpeas. Simmer, skimming occasionally until the chickpeas are tender, around two hours is usually sufficient. When cooked, season with salt and store the chickpeas in the cooking liquor until needed.

For The Loin

Heat a heavy frying pan or roasting tray over a high heat. Season the lamb with salt and place in the pan fat side down with the vegetable oil. When the fat has become nicely browned, turn the lamb over, add the garlic and thyme and put the pan into the oven at 180°C. Roast for about eight minutes, depending on the size of the loins, then remove the lamb to a cool tray. Pour over the garlic and thyme oil from the pan and leave it to rest on a warm plate for 15 to 20 minutes.

For The Garnish

Slice three of the radishes very thinly and reserve in iced water. Place the remaining radishes in a pan large enough to spread them in a single layer, add a knob of butter, a pinch of salt and sugar and cover them snugly with a sheet of kitchen parchment trimmed to fit the diameter of the pan. Cook the radishes until just tender then remove from the heat but leave in the pan. Cook the French beans in boiled salted water until tender then refresh in iced water and drain well when thoroughly cold.

To Serve

Assemble as in picture.

(see glossary)

Photographs by Jodi Hinds
www.jodihinds.com/blog Twitter: @jodihinds

CHAI PANNA COTTA, MANGO COMPOTE & COCONUT SORBET

SERVES 8

🍷 *Alsace Gewurztraminer Vdges Tardives: Rene Mure 2007 (France)*

Ingredients

Panna Cotta

15g cassia bark or cinnamon (broken into pieces)
10g cardamom pods (split)
10g Indian bay leaves (or European)
10g fresh ginger (finely grated)
600ml whipping cream
150ml milk
150g sugar
4 tsp loose tea (or 4 tea bags)
3 leaves gelatine (soaked in cold water for 10 minutes then drained well)

Mango Compote

2 or 3 mangoes (Indian Alfonso mangoes are best)
a little icing sugar
a little lime zest and juice (finely grated)
1 recipe of coconut sorbet
a few shavings from a fresh coconut for garnish

Coconut Biscuit

75g desiccated coconut
75g icing sugar
25g flour
60g egg white
50g butter (melted)

Coconut Sorbet

120ml water
120g sugar
400g coconut milk

Method

For The Panna Cotta

Heat a pan large enough for the cream and milk over a moderate heat. Toast the cinnamon and cardamom in the dry pan briefly until they become fragrant. Add the cream, milk, sugar and bay leaves. Bring to the boil and add the teas. Remove from the heat. Allow the tea and spices to infuse until you are happy with the strength of flavour (about six or eight minutes or longer if using tea bags).

Pass the warm mixture through the muslin or a fine sieve into a jug then pour into eight metal *dariole* moulds of about 80ml capacity. Chill in the fridge to set.

> **Chef's Tip**
> Don't forget the wobble.

For The Mango Compote And Coconut Biscuits

Peel the mango and dice the flesh. Add sugar, lime juice and zest to taste then reserve. Place all the ingredients for the biscuit mix into the bowl of a food processor and mix to a paste. Work in the melted butter for a few seconds until smooth. Spoon some of the mixture onto baking parchment and spread thinly with a palette knife.

Bake at 170°C until pale golden brown and crisp when cooled. Break the cooled biscuit into shards ready to garnish the panna cotta.

For The Sorbet

Bring the water and sugar to the boil, making sure all the sugar is dissolved. Mix the coconut milk with the sugar syrup and when cooled churn in an ice cream maker. Reserve in the freezer when ready.

To Serve

When the panna cotta are set, dip each mould briefly into hot water and slip them out, one onto each plate. Spoon a little mango compote next to each with some coconut shavings and a scoop of coconut sorbet. Finish with a piece of coconut biscuit.

(see glossary)

Photographs by Jodi Hinds
www.jodihinds.com/blog Twitter: @jodihinds

210
THE SWAN WITH TWO NECKS

Nantwich Road, Blackbrook, Staffordshire, ST5 5EH

01782 680 343
www.theswanwithtwonecks.co.uk

Following years of neglect, The Swan With Two Necks was transformed in 2007 by four school friends into a fashionable country pub with stylish décor and a warm ambiance not to be found for miles around. The iconic site was elevated to the position it truly deserved and immediately proved popular with the local community, who loved the option of a drink and a meal in the casual bar area or letting the fabulous waiting staff look after them in the restaurant.

The vision of freshly prepared food, made using local ingredients where practical, delivered in a relaxed setting was proved a success. Award-winning general manager Chris Childs used his background as a head chef to build a team focussed on quality food and an attention to detail that's seldom found in a country pub environment.

"I believe my passion for this business can be seen by the customers who come back time after time and this has been passed on to the staff. Pride in our work is what sets us apart and helped us to win Staffordshire's Contemporary Pub Of The Year 2011," says Chris.

The menu has a mixture of traditional pub classics and international cuisine too. The steak and ale pie with short crust pastry proves that people love comfort food when it's top quality and this has sat comfortably on the menu against osso bucco, scallops and marlin. We're constantly striving to exceed our guests' expectations.

Award-winning General Manager Chris Childs used his background as a head chef to build a team focussed on quality food and an attention to detail that's seldom found in a country pub environment.

BAKED FIELD MUSHROOMS WITH THYME & GARLIC, BLUE CHEESE SAUCE TOPPED WITH DRESSED WATERCRESS

SERVES 4

🍷 *Trewa Estate Carmenere*
(Chile)

Ingredients

Yorkshire Blue Cheese Sauce

125g Yorkshire blue cheese (grated)
250ml double cream
125ml milk
5g arrow root (mixed with a little cold water)
salt and cracked black pepper to season

To Cook The Mushrooms

12 medium sized field mushrooms
(peeled and stalks removed)
olive oil to drizzle
10 sprigs thyme (picked and chopped)
8 cloves garlic (crushed)
Maldon sea salt

To Serve

4 slices brioche
lightly dressed watercress

Method

To Prepare The Yorkshire Blue Cheese Sauce

Pour the milk and cream into a saucepan and bring to a boil. Gently stir the arrow root into the milk and cream until it thickens slightly.

Add the blue cheese and season to taste.

To Prepare The Mushrooms

Place the mushrooms onto a baking tray with the thyme and garlic. Drizzle with oil and bake in the oven for around eight minutes on 190°C. Turn the mushrooms at least once.

Remove from the oven and season lightly with Maldon sea salt. Set aside to cool.

To Serve

Drizzle the brioche with a little extra virgin olive oil and toast until golden brown.

Place three mushrooms on each slice of brioche and bake for a further three to four minutes.

Pour over the blue cheese sauce and garnish with a 25g wedge of the Yorkshire blue and some of the watercress.

CHARGRILLED PORK STEAK WITH CHIVE CROQUETTE BABY CARROTS, CALVADOS CREAM SAUCE, CARAMELISED APPLES & SEARED WHITE PUDDING

SERVES 4

 Runamok Chardonnay (Australia)

Ingredients

4 pork chops

Chive Croquettes
500g potatoes (diced)
50g chives (chopped)
Maldon sea salt to taste

Breading The Croquettes
50g seasoned plain flour
2 large eggs (beaten and seasoned)
60g seasoned Panko breadcrumbs
(very course breadcrumbs)

Calvados Cream Sauce
100ml chicken stock (homemade or a good
quality bought one)
50ml Calvados Berneroy
200ml double cream
1 fresh bay leaf (torn)

For The Carrots
30 Chantenay or baby carrots
$^1/_2$ an orange
1 tsp Demerara or light brown sugar
pinch of Maldon sea salt
1 fresh bay leaf

For The White Pudding
360g white pudding
pinch of Maldon sea salt

Method

Chive Croquettes

Boil the potatoes in water until they start to go soft and are ready to mash. Drain and return the pan onto a low heat to dry out completely.

Mash until free of lumps and chill for at least half an hour. Add the chopped chives and season. Mould the mashed potato into the shape of croquettes then coat in the flour, submerge in the beaten egg and then roll in the breadcrumbs. Repeat if necessary until well coated.

Calvados Cream Sauce

Reduce the chicken stock with the bay leaves by half. Add the Calvados and reduce by a further half. Add the double cream and reduce again until the consistency is medium thick and season if needed.

For The Baby Carrots

Trim the tops and scrub the carrots gently. Place into a saucepan and cover with water. Add the rest of the ingredients and boil until the carrots are slightly soft.

For The White Pudding

Peel the white pudding and cut it into cylindrical shapes. Cook in a dry pan with a little Maldon sea salt until crisp.

For The Pork Chops

Rub with a little oil and chargrill.

To Serve

Assemble your dish as in the picture.

BEETROOT FRANGIPANE WITH A POPPY SEED & GINGER ICE CREAM

SERVES 12

🍷 *Wild Wood Zinfandel Rosé, offsets the beetroot and especially spice from the ice cream (USA)*

Ingredients

Pastry

500g plain flour
100g icing sugar (sifted)
250g unsalted butter
zest of 1 lemon
2 large free range eggs

Frangipane

120g unsalted butter (softened)
120g icing sugar (sifted)
120g ground almonds
3 large free range eggs
4 tsp dark rum

Beetroot Jam

125g beetroot (peeled and grated)
125g caster sugar
125ml water
7g ginger (peeled and grated)
1/2 a red chilli

To Serve

1 scoop per portion of poppy seed
and ginger ice cream from
Cheshire Farm Ice Cream in Tattenhall

Method

To Prepare The Pastry

Mix the flour and chilled butter together using your fingertips until it resembles breadcrumbs. Mix in the rest of the ingredients apart from the egg. Make a well in the centre then add the eggs and knead together until smooth. Wrap the pastry in clingfilm and chill for one hour.

Roll out the pastry to line a flan ring with one inch of overhang and blind bake for 15 minutes. Once baked neatly cut off the pastry that is hanging over the top of the flan tin.

To Prepare The Frangipane

Using a large mixer with a whisk attachment. Mix the butter and the icing sugar together thoroughly. Gradually mix in the beaten egg by continuously whisking. Remove from the mixer and sieve in the flour and ground almonds. Fold them into the mixture and mix in well. Now add and stir in the rum.

Preparing The Beetroot Jam

Bring all the ingredients to a boil and simmer until all excess *liquor* has evaporated. Chill then blend until smooth.

Putting The Dish Together For Cooking

Line the bottom of the pastry case with the beetroot jam, pipe in the frangipane mix and bake in the oven at 170°C for 30 to 35 minutes.

To Serve

Cut into the desired portion size and serve with a scoop of poppy seed and ginger ice cream.

220
THE THREE HORSESHOES
INN & COUNTRY HOTEL

Buxton Road, Blackshaw Moor, Leek, Staffordshire, ST13 8TW

01538 300 296
www.3shoesinn.co.uk

Peacefully located on the edge of the Peak District National Park and within the Staffordshire Moorlands, The Three Horseshoes Inn And Country Hotel is an ideal location with its beautiful gardens, patios and stunning views over the Roaches and surrounding countryside.

Originally started by parents Bill and Jill Kirk in 1981, the business has been run by their sons, Mark and Stephen for the last ten years. For over 30 years the Kirk family have gained a wealth of experience to create a warm and relaxing atmosphere.

The Three Horseshoes Inn And Country Hotel offers three different dining experiences.

The Brasserie, with its open kitchen, wok cooking and large oak trussed ceiling, is ideal for relaxed and informal dining, offering an award-winning menu (two AA Rosettes and numerous Taste of Staffordshire awards) that combines modern English with Thai specialities.

The Bar Carvery And Grill offers a friendly, traditional pub atmosphere with log fires and oak beams.

Kirk's Restaurant is famous for its traditional Sunday lunch, themed event nights, Summer balls and Christmas parties. For private celebrations, Kirk's makes a popular venue for weddings and large private functions.

The hotel offers 26 stylish and distinctive bedrooms, from traditional cottage style rooms to contemporary executive and luxury bedrooms with massage showers or whirlpool baths making it the perfect place to stay.

'Award-Winning Local Food'
Chef Stephen Kirk and his team create award-winning, quality food using produce from local farmers, with a balance of knowledge and creativity offering a good choice of menus. This combination of high standards of service and value for money is the promise that the Inn and Hotel always strives to deliver and it is how it has gained its justifiable reputation as being one of Staffordshire's premier establishments.

ORIENTAL DUCK THREE WAYS
DUCK SPRING ROLL WITH TAMARIND FRUIT DIP; SHREDDED DUCK SALAD IN HOI SIN & SESAME; DUCK & PANCETTA STEAMED DIM SUM

SERVES 8

Gewurztraminer - Simonsig Estate - Stellenbosch (South Africa)

Ingredients

Crispy Duck

2 duck legs
1 tsp Chinese five spice
50g fresh ginger (chopped)
2 tbsp dark soy sauce
1tbsp Shaoxing rice wine
2 tbsp honey
1 tbsp vegetable oil
1 tbsp water

Salad For Crispy Duck

2 tbsp plum sauce
2 tbsp hoi sin
2 tbsp Shaoxing rice wine
2 tbsp water
200g watercress
1 cucumber (peeled, de-seeded and sliced)
5g sesame seeds (toasted)

Duck And Pancetta Dim Sum

1 duck leg meat
50g pancetta (diced)
zest of $1/2$ orange
1 tsp curry powder
1 tbsp plum sauce
1 egg white
salt
16 won ton wrappers

Duck Roll

1 duck leg
2 cloves garlic
1 carrot
1 small onion
100g diakon or white radish
20g Chinese five spice
20g Japanese pickled ginger
10ml light soy sauce
2 spring onions (chopped)
8 sheets spring roll wrappers (4 inch)
5g sea salt

Method

For The Crispy Duck

Mix all ingredients. Cover with foil and place in oven at 140°C for three hours until tender. Remove the foil, increase the temperature to 180°C and cook until the skin is crispy.

Prepare the salad dressing by mixing together the plum sauce, hoi sin, rice wine and water.

Remove the duck legs and allow them to cool slightly then pick the meat and skin from the bone and shred it.

For The Duck And Pancetta Dim Sum

Mince the duck leg meat and pancetta, then add plum sauce, orange zest and curry spice. Separately whisk the egg white to a firm peak. Fold the egg white into the meat mix. Season with salt. Place one teaspoon of the mixture into the centre of each wrap then fold over the four sides to form a dim sum.

For The Duck Roll

Purée the carrot, onion, garlic and diakon. Place the duck legs in a tray and rub the vegetable mixture into the meat, then add five spice and sea salt. Cover with foil and place in the oven at 110°C for four hours until the meat is very tender. Then, while still warm, flake off any meat. Discard any bones, sinew, skin and excess fats. Using both hands squeeze meat. Add chopped spring onions, chopped pickled ginger and soy sauce. Place in the fridge to go cold. Place a tablespoon of the mixture into the centre of a won ton wrapper. Form meat to make a cigar shape. Egg wash all edges of the wrapper. Fold over the two sides by 1cm and roll the meat in the pastry tightly to form a spring roll.

To Serve

Deep fry the spring rolls until golden. Steam the won tons for seven minutes until firm and cooked. Combine the watercress, dressing, cucumber and sesame seeds to make the salad.

Serve as shown with Tamarind dip.

POACHED STAFFORDSHIRE FREE RANGE BELLY PORK
BLACK PUDDING, BUBBLE & SQUEAK, PIG CHEEK & PRUNE CHIPOLATA, PORK SCRATCHING, SAGE JUS

SERVES 8

🍷 *Kotare - Pinot Noir - Marlborough (New Zealand)*

Ingredients

1 whole pork belly (boned, rolled and skin removed)
2 carrots
1 Spanish onion
3 sticks celery
100g leek
4 cloves garlic
2 tbsp sherry vinegar
2 tbsp light soy sauce
1 litre good chicken stock
75g black pudding

Bubble And Squeak
400g potatoes (cooked)
3 carrots (cooked)
100g green cabbage (cooked)
100g frozen peas
1 small onion (diced)
2 eggs
25ml double cream
50g plain flour

Pig Cheek And Prune Chipolata
4 slices prosciutto (halved)
8 dried prunes (soaked in brandy)
50ml veal stock
1 sprig thyme
1 sprig sage
2 pig cheeks
2 cloves fresh garlic

Sage Jus
10 shallots
50ml extra virgin olive oil
2 sprigs thyme
4 sprigs sage
500ml dry cider
1 litre good chicken stock

Method

For The Pork Belly
Brown all sides of the joint in a hot pan then remove and set aside. Using the same pan, sauté the remaining vegetables until softened. *Deglaze* the pan with sherry vinegar then return the joint to the pan and cover with chicken stock and soy sauce. Cover and simmer for two and a half to three hours. When ready the meat should be tender but with some resistance. Reserve the pork stock for the sage *jus*. Cut into eight portions.

For The Sage Jus
Sweat chopped shallots in the olive oil and herbs until they are soft but not coloured. Add cider and reduce until it has a syrupy consistency. Add the sauce from the pork and the chicken stock and reduce again, this time by two thirds. Pass the liquid through a sieve.

For The Bubble And Squeak
Bash all the vegetables together. Fry the onion in a pan and add to the vegetables. Season with salt and pepper then mix in the flour, egg and cream to combine. Line a deep tray with parchment paper then add the mix to 3cm deep. Place in the oven and cook at 150°C for about one hour. Check at regular intervals. Cut into eight portions with 6cm ring cutter.

> **Chef's Tip**
> Instead of cooking fresh vegetables for the bubble and squeak, make it the traditional way and use any vegetables leftover from your Sunday roast.

For The Pig Cheek And Prune Chipolata
Preheat the oven to 130°C. Add the stock, cheeks, herbs and garlic to a deep tray. Cover with foil and place in the oven. Cook slowly for two to three hours until the cheeks are tender. Remove the cheeks then reduce the stock to produce a thick glaze.

Break up cheeks to form a paste, then add the reduced stock and seasoning. Allow to cool.

Lay sheets of ham on board. Spread some of the pig cheek over half of the sheet, add prune then tightly roll.

To Serve
Place the meat portions into the sauce and complete by braising in the sauce, turning half way until fully glazed and hot; remove from the sauce. Discard the string. Fry black pudding in a little oil. Serve as in the photo with crispy pork crackling.

PINEAPPLE & PINK PEPPERCORN TARTE TATIN

SERVES 4

🍷 *Stone Paddock Isabella Late Harvest Semillon (New Zealand)*

Ingredients

Pineapple And Pink Peppercorn Tarte Tatin

600g super sweet pineapple
8 tbsp caster sugar
4 tbsp unsalted butter
4 tsp water
4 tsp pink peppercorns (crushed)
400g all butter puff pastry

Coconut Milk Sorbet

600ml coconut milk
200ml water
200g caster sugar
50g glucose liquid

Method

For The Coconut Milk Sorbet

Bring the water and sugar to the boil whilst stirring continuously until the sugar is dissolved. Allow the syrup to cool. Add coconut milk and glucose and stir. Churn in an ice cream machine until frozen although be careful not to over-churn. Place into the freezer until required.

For The Pineapple And Pink Peppercorn Tarte Tatin

Cut the pineapple into rings, approximately one inch in depth, and remove the core. Melt the butter, sugar and water in four small, 4 - 5" pans to produce a golden caramel. Add the peppercorns when the caramel is ready. Add the pineapple and cook until it has caramelised then set it aside until ready to serve. Roll the puff pastry and cut into four disks to fit the size of the pans. Reserve until ready.

Chef's Tip

Try making a Tarte Tatin with different fruits such as apples, pears or bananas.

To Serve

Assemble the pastry disc on top of the caramelised pineapple. Roll in edges. Bake in a preheated oven for approximately 15 minutes at 190°C until the pastry is golden. Ensure pastry is fully cooked before serving. Serve with a scoop of the coconut milk sorbet.

230
TURNERS

69 High Street, Harborne, Birmingham, B17 9NS

0121 426 4440
www.turnersrestaurantbirmingham.co.uk

When The New York Times named Birmingham as one of the best places in the world to visit for food, it did so because of chefs like Richard Turner.

The Michelin-starred chef's eponymous restaurant was cited by the influential publication as being a must-visit destination. It included Turners with good reason. Richard Turner is an exceptional chef, whose impressive technical skills are allied to a strong creative streak.

Those qualities have been recognised by numerous culinary movers and shakers down the years. Turners was awarded a Michelin Star in 2009 and retained the accolade in 2010, 2011 and 2012. It has achieved high marks from the Good Food Guide in all of those years, and was runner up in Hardens Guide Best Newcomer 2010. Turners was also included in the Sunday Times Top 100 Restaurants for 2011/12.

"I am deeply passionate about great food," says Richard. "We are not afraid to embrace new techniques, but the important thing to us is to let the natural flavours shine through."

Turners has been central to Birmingham's culinary renaissance. The neighbourhood bijou venue, in the suburb of Harborne, has a loyal clientele and has become a destination restaurant that attracts people from around the UK.

Richard leads a close brigade and makes sure his staff pay every attention to detail. "The standards have to be as high as possible. We never rest on our laurels. We are always pushing to improve. We are restless, we want to be the best we can."

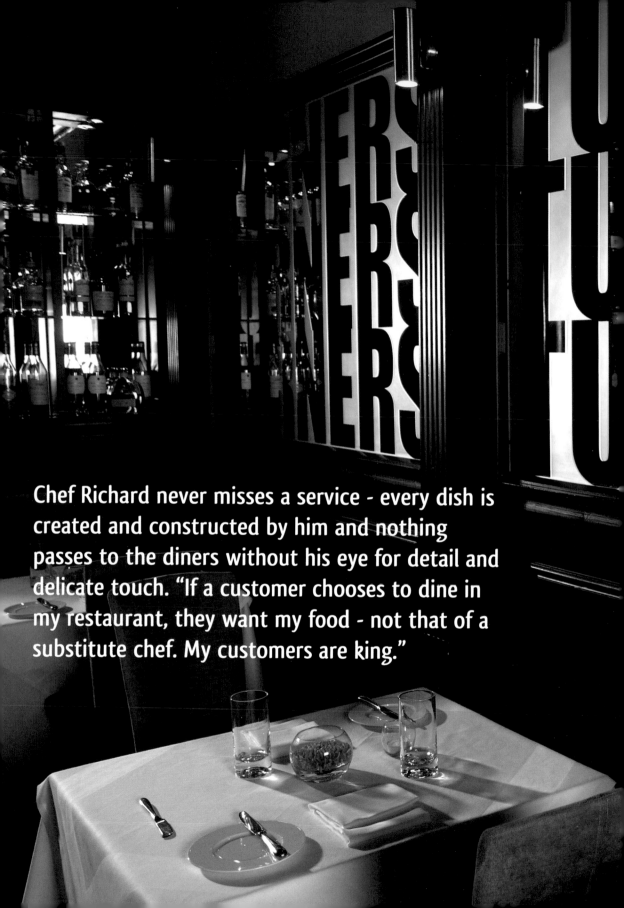

Chef Richard never misses a service - every dish is created and constructed by him and nothing passes to the diners without his eye for detail and delicate touch. "If a customer chooses to dine in my restaurant, they want my food - not that of a substitute chef. My customers are king."

HAND DIVED SCALLOPS, MI-CUIT AVOCADO PUREE, SOYA & HONEY DRESSING, HORSERADISH SNOW

SERVES 4

Sake. Akashi -Tai Honjozo
(Japan)

Ingredients

Scallops

12 hand dived scallops
sea salt
caster sugar
coriander seeds
1 lime (grated zest)
lemon oil

Avocado Purée

2 ripe avocados
1 lemon (juice)
salt and pepper

Soya And Honey Dressing

1 egg yolk
25g white wine vinegar
25g Dijon mustard
500ml Pomace olive oil
25ml of clear honey
50g of light soya sauce (reduced by half)

Horseradish Snow

500g of buttermilk
75g grated horseradish
15g cornflour
90g milk
lemon juice and salt

Garnish

mixed oriental leaves
bunch of breakfast radishes

Method

For The Horseradish Snow

Boil the milk and thicken with cornflour. Cool and set aside.
Add the buttermilk and horseradish and infuse for eight hours.
Pass through a fine sieve and season with lemon juice and salt to taste.

Place in a shallow plastic container and place in freezer.
When the mixture starts to freeze, scrape using a fork to give the appearance of snow.

For The Soya And Honey Dressing

Whisk the egg yolk, with white wine vinegar and the Dijon mustard. Slowly pour in the Pomace oil, continuing to whisk until it becomes the same consistency of mayonnaise and season with the honey and reduced soya sauce. Add salt and pepper.

For The Avocado Purée

Peel the avocados and place in food processor. Purée on a high speed. Season with lemon juice and salt to taste.

For The Scallops

Mix the salt, sugar and coriander seeds in a grinder. Season scallops with the salt and sugar mix then add grated fresh lime zest. Heat the lemon oil to 48°C, and poach the scallops in the oil for six minutes. Remove and drain on a kitchen towel.

For The Serve

As shown in picture. Place three scallops on each plate, garnish with avocado purée, sliced radish and Chinese herbs. Sprinkle with horseradish snow.

> **Chef's Tip**
>
> I like to use hand-dived scallops because they are the best quality. The scallops are served mi-cuit, which means they are half-cooked.

TASTING OF CORNISH LAMB, RED PEPPERS, GOATS CHEESE GNOCCHI, ROCKET PESTO, LAMB JUS

SERVES 4

Château de Pez 2006, St Estephe, Cru Bourgeois Exceptional (France)

Ingredients

For The Lamb Shoulder
1kg lamb shoulder
1ltr chicken stock
1 onion, carrot, leek
1 bouquet garni

For The Lamb Belly
1 lamb belly (rolled)
1 carrot, leek, onion
1 packet feuille de brick (pastry)

For The Lamb Loin
1 lamb loin
4 lamb sweetbreads

Peppers And Stuffed Aubergine
4 red peppers
4 plum tomatoes (blanched, peeled and deseeded)
1 garlic clove
1 aubergine
1 sprig rosemary
1 shallot

Rocket Pesto
50ml olive oil, rocket, parmesan and garlic

Lamb Jus
500ml veal stock
250ml Madeira
10ml vinegar
250g shallots
250g button mushrooms
1 head of garlic

Gnocchi
500g Désirée potatoes
75g 00 pasta flour
1 egg
40g goat's cheese
pinch of salt

Method

For The Lamb
Seal the lamb shoulder in a hot pan and then braise with the vegetables, bouquet garni and the chicken stock until tender.

Cook the lamb belly as above. Strain the liquor then roll the belly in clingfilm. Place in the fridge to set. Flake the lamb shoulder, add some of the reduced cooking liquid and then wrap with the feuille de brick.

Seal the lamb loin, belly and sweetbreads in a frying pan and cook in an oven at 180°C for five minutes then rest.

For The Peppers And Stuffed Aubergine
Cut the peppers into julienne and cook with the tomato, shallot and garlic. Cut the aubergine in half, score with a criss-cross and stuff with garlic, rosemary and olive oil. Wrap in tin foil and bake in the oven at 180°C for 35 minutes, peel and roughly chop.

For The Rocket Pesto
Purée the rocket, olive oil, garlic and parmesan, purée in a food processor.

For The Gnocchi
Bake the Désirée potatoes in the oven. When cooked, peel and purée, take 300g and mix with goat's cheese, egg, flour and salt to form a dough. Roll out into little balls and shape with a fork. Blanch in boiling water and the refresh in iced water.

For The Jus
Add the shallots, button mushrooms and the garlic to the frying pan used earlier for the meat and *deglaze* with the vinegar and Madeira. Reduce to a syrup, add the veal stock and reduce again. Pass through a fine sieve.

To Serve
Place the aubergine and rocket purée on the plate, carve a piece of the lamb loin alongside the sweetbread and the belly. Place the deep fried lamb shoulder on the side and garnish with the gnocchi, red pepper and pesto. Finally, pour the sauce around the edge as in picture.

> **Chef's Tip**
> Let the meat rest for at least 15 minutes at room temperature wrapped in foil.

VANILLA CREME BRULEE, STRAWBERRY, HONEYCOMB, BASIL, WHITE BALSAMIC FOAM

SERVES 4

🍷 *Sauternes. Chateau De la Chartreuse,*
South Quest 2006 (France)

Ingredients

Crème Brûlée

4 egg yolks
190ml double cream
63ml milk
37.5g caster sugar
demerara sugar for sprinkling (and a blow torch)

Honeycomb

200g caster sugar
100ml still bottled water
2 tsp bicarbonate of soda

White Balsamic Foam

125ml white balsamic vinegar
62ml bottled still water
62ml stock syrup (half sugar to water)
4 gelatine leaves

Garnish

1 punnet of strawberries
Thai basil
strawberry sorbet
strawberry coulis

Method

For The Brûlée

Bring the cream and milk to the boil over a medium high heat in a heavy-bottomed pan. Allow to cool slightly. Whisk the egg yolks and sugar together, then pour the warmed cream and milk mixture over. Strain the liquid and pour into ramekins. Bake in oven at 100°C for 25 to 30 minutes until lightly set. Cool to room temperature.

For The Balsamic Foam (Optional)

Bring water and syrup to the boil. Add soaked gelatine leaves to the liquid. Pass through a fine sieve and add to white balsamic. Set in an 'Isi' bottle charged with two gasses. Some cooks may find this a little complicated. Do not worry if you have to skip this stage, but it is worthwhile if you can.

For The Honeycomb

Gently heat the caster sugar and water in a large heavy-bottomed pan, until the sugar has dissolved. Now turn up the heat and boil, without stirring. Do not allow it to go too dark as it will become bitter. Swirl the mixture, without stirring, to achieve an even colour. Now add the bicarbonate of soda, which will make the mixture fizz and expand. Tip into an oiled baking tin and leave to cool, until set

To Serve

Turn the brûlée out of the ramekin, glaze with demerara sugar and a blow torch. Place on serving plate and garnish with the sorbet, strawberry coulis, Thai basil and honeycomb.

> **Chef's Tip**
> Best not to place in fridge - cool naturally to retain flavours.

240
THE WARWICK
RESTAURANT BRASSERIE

Stratford Road, Hockley Heath, Warwickshire, B94 5NW

01564 785 252
www.warwickhockleyheath.co.uk

The Warwick, recently renamed, is a venue which offers diverse dining within its impressive converted Tithe barn, that once held the local food market. European dishes are fused with regional produce and their ingredients are largely sourced from within the county. Warwickshire is renowned for its quality meats, artisan suppliers and arable farmers, one of which is located next door, and supplies much of their produce to the restaurant. Classic aged British steaks, sit alongside Italian pasta and Mezzo and Spanish meatballs. The Warwick's fresh fish is sourced from the Birmingham fish market and is uniquely served in a Mediterranean style.

Al fresco dining is a major part of The Warwick's offering, providing the British Summer weather matches the Mediterranean influenced menu. A large griddle BBQ provides La Planch style cooking on the traditional, flat top grill serving their steaks, fresh fish and marinated kebabs to be enjoyed on their impressive decking area, beautifully lit in the evenings, and a popular haunt for the great and the good of the area.

The team who operate The Warwick have an impressive pedigree, with links to Terence Conran, Harvey Nichols, The Savoy and The Waldorf in New York. There is a depth of experience which applies itself to the considered service and consistent quality cuisine, balanced with the opulent setting, which makes The Warwick a must visit.

Photographs by Sam Bagnall

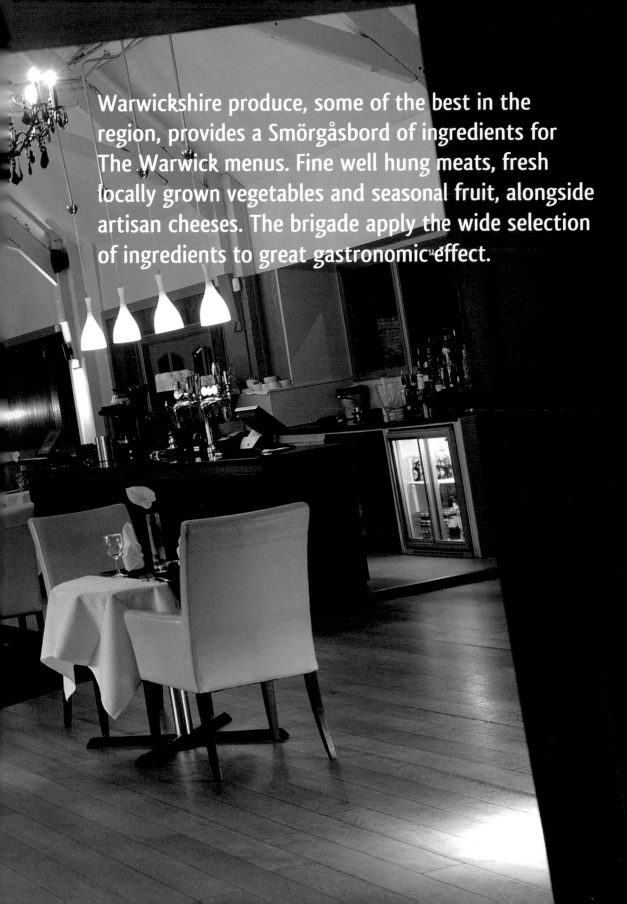

Warwickshire produce, some of the best in the region, provides a Smörgåsbord of ingredients for The Warwick menus. Fine well hung meats, fresh locally grown vegetables and seasonal fruit, alongside artisan cheeses. The brigade apply the wide selection of ingredients to great gastronomic effect.

KING SCALLOPS 'ON BLACK' WITH PARSNIPS

SERVES 1 (RECIPE BASED ON PER PERSON)

 Young Loire Sauvignon Blanc (New Zealand)

Ingredients

3 king scallops (per person)
3 slices black pudding (per person)
butter
olive oil
4 parsnips
300ml milk
300ml double cream
sparkling/soda water (to clean scallops)

Method

For The Scallops

Remove roe and sinew from scallops. Use sparkling water to remove the grit and dirt from the scallops as this gently cleans them. Dry on a clean towel.

Bring frying pan up to a very high heat. Add oil then add the scallops and turn after one minute on each side. Finish with a knob of butter before removing.

Chef's Tip

Use sparkling water as this removes the dirt without the need for rubbing the scallop.

For The Parsnip Purée

Peel four parsnips and cover with milk and cream (50:50 ratios) keep stirring to avoid catching on pan. Bring to the boil and cook until tender. Once cooked blend until smooth and pass through a sieve.

For The Black Pudding

Panfry black pudding slices in olive oil until heated through.

To Serve

Assemble as in the picture.

WARWICKSHIRE 'CRACKLING' BELLY PORK WITH PANFRIED BLACK PUDDING & 'PROPER' MASH

SERVES 4

🍷 *Beaujolais Villages (France)*
Not too old and served very lightly chilled.

Ingredients

1kg pork belly (skin on)
2 carrots
2 celery sticks
1 onion (roughly chopped)
black pudding (good quality)
2 Granny Smith apples
pinch of sugar
juice of ¹/₂ lemon
1 pint red wine
2 shallots (finely chopped)
water

Chef's Tip

Separate the skin after the first cook and cook on high with some salt to make seriously good crackling.

Method

To Prepare The Pork Belly – The Day Before

Cook on a bed of mire-poix vegetables (carrots, celery and onion). Place the pork belly on these vegetables with a pint of water poured over. Cover with greaseproof paper over the belly. Lay a medium to heavy baking tray on top of the belly to stop it rising and curling during the cooking.

Cook on 175°C for 40 minutes and then 155°C for one hour.

When the pork is tender, set aside to cool with the tray on top and press with a greater weight overnight. A belly the size of an A4 sheet needs approximately four tins of beans in weight on top.

Remove pork belly and **keep** the vegetables and stock.

Once pressed remove the skin, the salt and then cook the skin on the top shelf at 185°C for five minutes until crispy. Heat the belly meat on the lower shelf in the same oven to serve.

For The Apple Purée

Heat two Granny Smith apples, peeled cored and roughly chopped, with a dash of water and with the juice of half a lemon. Add a good pinch of sugar. Constantly stir to avoid it from sticking to the bottom of the pan. When the apples are soft and still have no colour, blend until smooth then cool.

For The Black Pudding

Panfry black pudding slices in olive oil until heated through.

For The Mash

Bring peeled potatoes to the boil in heavily salted water. Once boiled, drain and repeat in clean unsalted water. This will keep mash less starchy and have better flavour. When cooked, drain and push through a ricer (or mash until smooth). Add butter and seasoning and beat with a spoon or spatula until smooth in texture.

For The Sauce

Reduce the red wine over chopped shallots, then add the strained cooking *liquor* from the pork belly and vegetables. Reduce this further until thick. Season to taste.

To Serve

Assemble as in the picture.

RELISH MIDLANDS **THE WARWICK**

(see glossary)
Photographs by Sam Bagnall

WARWICK CHOCOLATE BROWNIE TRUFFLES & CHOCOLATE SAUCE

SERVES 12 OR A GREEDY 6! (KEEP IN AN AIRTIGHT CONTAINER)

 Brown Brothers Orange Muscat
(Australia) Serve slightly chilled.

Ingredients

Brownie
250g dark chocolate
250g butter
300g golden caster sugar
3 large, free range eggs plus one extra yolk
60g self raising flour
60g cocoa powder
$^1/_2$ teaspoon baking powder
pinch salt

Chocolate Sauce
$^2/_3$ cup unsweetened cocoa
$^2/_3$ cup white sugar
$1^1/_4$ cups water
1 tsp vanilla extract

Chocolate Truffles
150ml double cream
100 - 120g chocolate (broken into small pieces)
cocoa powder (to dust the truffles)
1 banana and a handful of pistachios (optional)

Chef's Tip
If you want to add nuts or any other bits and pieces, add them to the mixture immediately after you have stirred in the melted chocolate. Nothing beats looking at chocolates you have made.

Method

For The Brownie
Preheat the oven to 180°C/350°F.

Grease a 23cm x 23cm/9" x 9" non-stick baking tin and line the bottom with baking paper.

Cream the butter and sugar together until white, fluffy and creamy, either by hand or in the food processor. Break the chocolate into pieces and melt all of it in a bowl in a *bain-marie*. (except for 50g). Remove from the heat as soon as it has melted. Chop the remaining 50g of chocolate into small chunks.

Beat the eggs in a small bowl and then beat gradually into the butter and sugar mix. Stir in the melted chocolate and the remaining 50g of chocolate chunks with a metal spoon.
Sift together flour and baking powder, cocoa and salt and then fold this carefully into the batter with a metal spoon. Turn the mixture into the cake tin, smooth the top and bake for about 30 minutes.

It is important not to overcook brownies or they will be dry and lose that moist, chewy texture that is their hallmark. So check after 25 minutes. The top should have risen but it will appear softer in the middle. Test with a skewer in the middle. It should come out a bit sticky but not with liquid raw mix on it. If it does, put back in for another three minutes and check again. You don't want the skewer to come out clean.

For The Chocolate Sauce
Combine cocoa, sugar and water. Bring to a boil for one minute. Remove from heat and stir in vanilla.

For The Chocolate Truffles
Bring the cream to a boil. Turn off the heat add the chocolate pieces immediately. Keep stirring until all the chocolate has melted. Place in *bain-marie* if there are any lumps. Place in a bowl in the fridge until solid. Best left overnight.

Option: Pour half the mixture into the tin and add, on top, a layer of banana, pistachios, or even more chocolate. Then add the remainder of the chocolate - you'll have your chosen ingredient all through the middle.

Lay the chocolate truffle mix into a tray and allow to cool. Once cool, use a knife, warmed up in hot water, to cut into cubes and dust.

To Serve
Assemble as in picture - a high quality brandy snap can be bought from local speciality food shops. Add ice cream of your choice.

(see glossary)
Photographs by Sam Bagnall

250
THE WAYFARER

The Wayfarer Stone, The Fillybrooks, Stone, Staffordshire, ST15 0NB

01785 811 023
www.thewayfarerstone.co.uk

The Wayfarer has been a landmark pub for many years but never has it had such a radical revitalisation like the refurbishment that has just been completed as of the end of 2011 under its new, independent owners. Interior designers have brought the latest styles and combined them with reassuring, familiar elements to create a scheme that is both exciting and current whilst retaining a relaxed and inviting atmosphere. Sumptuous fabrics combine with distressed leather on the furniture. Rustic woods and forged steel give a mix of textures, bringing nature and industry into the pub for the first time in this region.

Carefully thought out recipes are lovingly prepared from the freshest ingredients. The creative kitchen team have taken their favourites from dining out over the years and formulated an interesting and unique menu. Their interpretation of a Chinese favourite, crispy duck, is enormously popular for instance, but traditional tastes are also catered for with locally sourced steaks and homemade pub classics. There are also handmade stone baked pizzas that rival the best you can find on the continent.

Whether it's a seat in the bar, where we stock four traditional cask ales and four lagers to give a great choice for beer lovers, or a table in our private dining area for an intimate dinner with friends, you'll be sure of a warm welcome.

farer

Carefully thought out recipes are lovingly prepared from the freshest ingredients. The creative kitchen team have taken their favourites from dining out over the years and formulated an interesting and unique menu.

POTTED CORNISH CRAB WITH WHOLEMEAL TOAST

SERVES 4

Benchmark Chardonnay as crab is one of fuller flavoured shellfish. (Australia)

Ingredients

Potted Crab

1 medium Cornish brown crab
(your fish supplier should be able to supply you
with the meat already prepared out of the shell
if you prefer this to cooking and shelling the
crab yourself)
juice from $^1/_2$ lemon (pips removed)
pinch of seasoning

Butter Topping

1 banana shallot (finely diced)
25ml Harvey's Bristol Cream sherry
small pinch cayenne pepper
small pinch fresh nutmeg
100g butter
1 tbsp Worcestershire sauce
juice from $^1/_2$ lemon (pips removed)

To Serve

4 slices of wholemeal bread
salad leaves
1 lemon (quartered)

Method

To Prepare The Crab

Mix the white and brown crab meat together, removing any small bones.

Add the juice from half of the lemon and a pinch of seasoning.

Half fill a small Kilner jar with the mix.

To Prepare The Butter Topping

Gently cook the shallots in butter then add the remaining ingredients and heat through slowly for a few minutes or until the butter has taken on all the flavours. Drain through a sieve.

Cover the crab with about a tablespoon of butter and leave in the fridge only long enough to set the butter, try not let it go too cold.

To Serve

Toast the bread and present neatly on a plate next to the potted crab. Serve with a wedge of lemon and some salad leaves dressed lightly with extra virgin olive oil and Maldon sea salt.

ROASTED BELLY PORK WITH CARAMELISED APPLE SAUCE, BABY CARROTS & NEW POTATOES

SERVES 4

🍷 *Featherdrop Hill Pinot Noir
(New Zealand)*

Ingredients

To Braise The Pork Belly

1kg pork belly (boned, rolled and tied.
The butcher will bone and roll this for
you if you ask)
2 litres of chicken stock (preferably homemade or
a good quality bought one)

Apple Chutney

2 Granny Smith apples (peeled, cored and diced)
50g Demerara or light brown sugar
1 bay leaf
2 sprigs thyme

Apple And Sage Sauce

2 Granny Smith apples (peeled, cored and diced)
6 large leaves of sage (chopped)
500ml stock from braising the pork belly
200ml double cream

Vegetables For Serving

20 Chantenay carrots
10 new potatoes (cut into halves)
4 large handfuls washed spinach
4 large fresh bay leaves for garnishing

Method

Braising The Belly Pork

Place the pork belly in a deep roasting dish and pour over
the chicken stock. Then cover with tin foil, place in an oven
preheated to 120°C and cook for six hours.

> **Chef's Tip**
>
> When the pork is cooked, cool completely then roll in
> clingfilm and refrigerate for eight hours. This will keep the
> pork belly in shape for roasting.

Slice the pork belly into four portions.

For The Apple Chutney

Add all ingredients and cook on a low temperature for around
20 minutes until a jam consistency is reached.

For The Apple And Sage Sauce

Place 500mm of the pork stock in a saucepan and reduce by two
thirds. Add the cream and reduce by a further third then add the
chopped sage and diced apple. Cook for a further eight minutes.
Season to taste.

Preparing The Dish For Service

Place the pork belly into a frying pan with a splash of vegetable
oil and fry until golden brown on all sides. Place in a preheated
oven at 200°C for 15 minutes until hot.

Par boil the carrots and potatoes and place in the oven at the
same time as the pork with a knob of butter. Heat the apple and
sage sauce in a pan ready to serve.

Heat a pan with a very small splash of oil and flash fry the
spinach. Drain any moisture from it.

To Serve

Plate as seen in the picture.

LEMON TART WITH CHANTILLE CREAM & FRESH RASPBERRIES

SERVES 12

🍷 *Orange Muscat & Flora*
(Australia)

Ingredients

Pastry

250g plain flour
100g butter
100g icing sugar
seeds from 1 vanilla pod

Filling

8 egg yolks
4 whole eggs
360g caster sugar
400ml cream
juice of 4 lemons
zest of 2 lemons

Garnish

300ml whipped cream
60g of icing sugar (whipped into the cream)
fresh raspberries for garnishing (3 per portion)

Method

To Prepare The Pastry

Mix all the pastry ingredients together, except the egg, using your fingertips until it resembles breadcrumbs. Make a well in the centre then add the eggs and knead together until smooth. Wrap in clingfilm and chill for one hour.

Roll out the pastry to line a flan ring with roughly one inch of overhang and blind bake for 15 minutes. Once baked, neatly cut off the pastry that is hanging over the flan tin.

To Prepare The Filling

Mix the eggs and sugar together until smooth then add the cream, lemon juice and zest. Whisk thoroughly and pour into the pastry case, bake for 30 to 40 minutes at 120°C until set.

To Serve

Cut into the desired portion size. Place neatly on a plate with some whipped cream and some of the fresh raspberries.

260
RELISH MIDLANDS LARDER

BAKERY

CHURCH FARM HOUSE CAKES

Church Farm House, Middle Street, Croxton Kerrial,
Grantham, Lincolnshire, NG31 1QP.
01476 870 150
www.churchfarmhousecakes.co.uk

*The successful and renowned company Church Farm House
Cakes is an award-winning cake business - their brandy
fruit cake and almond fruit cake having won gold from
The Guild of Fine Food Awards and they were finalists in
The Telegraph and Waitrose Small Food Producer of the
Year Awards.*

CLAYBROOKE MILL (FLOURS)

Frolesworth Lane, Claybrooke Magna,
Leicestershire, LE17 5DB.
01455 202 443
www.claybrookewatermill.co.uk

*Claybrooke Mill is the only commercially working water mill
in Leicestershire, still milling most days using water power.
They produce a range of organic flours and flour mixes,
using traditional equipment, some of which is hundreds of
years old.*

ELIZABETH'S PATISSERIE

18 Lowater Street, Carlton, Nottingham, NG4 1JJ.
0115 987 2058
www.elizabethspatisserie.co.uk

*Family business founded in 1860, all products are hand
made using traditional methods at their local bakery in
Nottingham. They offer a variety of speciality and Polish
continental breads and a selection of cakes and pastries.*

HAMBLETON BAKERY

Cottesmore Road, Exton, Oakham, Rutland LE15 8AN.
01572 812 995
www.hambletonbakery.co.uk

*In September 2008, Julian Carter and Tim Hart opened
Hambleton Bakery to produce top quality, traditionally
made bread for Hambleton Hall and Hart's Nottingham.
In addition to a growing list of wholesale customers (pubs,
restaurants, delis, etc) the bakery now has retail outlets in
Exton, Stamford and Oakham.*

KINGS ROAD BAKERY

21 Kings Road, Melton Mowbray, Leicestershire LE13 1QF.
01664 410 065
www.kingsroadbakery.co.uk

*Melton Mowbray's only remaining independent craft
bakery, making quality breads without additions of
chemicals, with the taste and consistency that was found
back in mother's day.*

SWIFTS BAKERY

High Street, Clee Hill, Ludlow, Shropshire, SY8 3LZ.
01584 890 003
www.swifts.bakery.co.uk

*Swifts Bakery pride themselves on being a craft baker, with
the emphasis on craft. The art of making a loaf of bread is
something that should never be forgotten. They create their
dough from scratch and use a wide range of flours and only
the freshest ingredients.*

BEVERAGES

BELVOIR BREWERY
Crown Park, Station Road, Old Dalby,
Leicestershire, LE14 3NQ.
01664 823 455
www.belvoirbrewery.co.uk

The original Belvoir Brewery (pronounced 'Beaver') was set up in 1995. The brewery was constructed using mostly original equipment and artefacts recovered from traditional cask ale breweries all over the country.

CELTIC MARCHES BEVERAGES LTD
Wyer Croft, Bishops Frome, Worcester, WR6 5BS.
01684 569 142
www.celticmarches.com

Producers of high quality liqueurs and spirits with unique, innovative, eye catching packaging. Each bottle is hand finished in wax by an illustrious head waxer.

FLIPSIDE BREWERY LTD
The Brewhouse, East Link Trade Centre, Private Road No. 2, Colwick, Nottingham, Nottinghamshire, NG4 2JR.
0115 987 7500
www.flipsidebrewery.co.uk

Flipside Brewery supply many local pubs with their beers as well as the general public. They are one of many craft brewers of British ales to be found in Nottinghamshire and indeed, across the country.

GWATKIN CIDER CO
Moorhampton Park Farm, Abbey Dore,
Herefordshire, HR2 0AL.
01981 550 258
www.gwatkincider.co.uk

Producers of award-winning cider and perry.

JOHN VILLAR WINES
Steppes House, Wigmore, Herefordshire, HR6 9UA.
01568 770 191
www.johnvillarwines.co.uk

Supplier of high quality wines to hotels and restaurants, but also to a number of private customers.

PERFECT TIPPLE LIMITED
Orbital Plaza, Watling Street, Bridgtown, Cannock,
Staffordshire, WS11 0EL.
0121 288 7077
www.perfecttipple.co.uk

Sparkling Gold Cuvee is a unique award-winning sparkling wine, infused with real 23 carat gold flakes. This sparkling wine is sheer luxury and simply perfect for any occasion. Sparkling Gold Cuvee puts that extra special touch of class to your celebration.

RADNOR HILLS MINERAL WATER CO
Heartsease, Knighton, Powys, LD7 1LU.
01547 530 220
www.radnorhills.co.uk

Radnor Hills are suppliers of various mineral waters and soft drinks that are available from wholesalers throughout the UK.

TANNERS WINES
26 Wyle Cop, Shrewsbury, Shropshire, SY1 1XD.
01743 234 500
www.tanners-wines.co.uk

Wines from all corners of the world are available from this nationwide wine merchant.

UPTON WINES
8 New Street, Upton-upon-Severn, Worcester,
Worcestershire, WR8 0HR.
01684 592 668
www.uptonwines.co.uk

Family owned by father Alan and son Andy Goadby. Supplying individually selected wines from around the globe, specifically sourced for some of the Midlands, and UK's finest restaurants. Their bijou shop in picturesque Upon on Severn is worth a trip for any aficionado.

CONFECTIONERY

BONBONNIERE HANDMADE ORGANIC CHOCOLATES
Acton House, Underdale Road, Shrewsbury, SY2 5DG
www.bonbonniere.co.uk

Melanie Fallon is a self taught artisan chocolatier with a difference. Creating a bespoke handmade chocolate selection, including her famous chocolate slippers. Chocolate with style, created for individuals, and boutique hotels and restaurants.

DANIEL'S DELIGHTS
Units 7A and 8A, Oldham Street, Hanley, Stoke on Trent, Staffordshire, ST1 3EY.
01782 279 866
www.daniels-delights.co.uk

Expert chocolatiers, creating the finest truffles from the rare chocolate Callebaut.

FRANCES CRUTE
Shottery Road, Stratford-Upon-Avon,
Warwickshire, CV37 9QB.
07980 001 636
www.francescrute.co.uk

Frances Crute Chocolatiers create handmade chocolates using the finest ingredients.

HELSHAM CHOCOLATES
07803 137 835
www.helsham.co.uk

Helsham Chocolates was started in Leicester in 2009 to cater to the growing market for high quality handmade chocolates and truffles. They take a no compromise approach to ingredients, sourcing the finest flavours available.

DAIRY

BROCK HALL FARM DAIRY GOATS CHEESES
Chelmarsh, Bridgnorth, Shropshire WV16 6QA.
01746 862 533
www.brockhallfarm.com

Sarah Hampton is as passionate about her produce as they come - tending to her flock of pedigree goats, who produce a range of unique and wonderful artisan cheeses, fed on the green fields of the Shropshire countryside.

THE CHEESE SHOP
6 Flying Horse Walk, St Peters Gate, Nottingham, NR1 2HN.
01159 419 114
www.cheeseshop-nottingham.co.uk

Family run delicatessen, situated in the heart of Nottingham city centre. The shop was founded nearly two decades ago and specialises in selling cheese. They have developed their range throughout the years and now stock over 200 British cheeses from a wide variety of milks including cows, sheep, goats and buffalo.

CHURCHFIELDS FARMHOUSE ICE CREAM
Churchfields Farm, Salwarpe, Droitwich,
Worcestershire, WR9 0AH.
01905 451 289
www.churchfields-farm.co.uk

Award-winning ice cream, the perfect balance of freshness, lightness and creaminess, carefully judged with a mix of milk and double cream. Churchfields has a denser more rounded texture. It is deliciously creamy, without being rich or cloying.

CROPWELL BISHOP CREAMERY
Nottingham Road, Cropwell Bishop, Nottingham, NG12 3BQ.
01159 892 350
www.cropwellbishopstilton.com

With more than 160 years of cheese making experience, you could say that the Skailes family has blue blood in its veins. Whichever way you look at it, they certainly have an enviable heritage when it comes to producing delicious and award-winning cheese.

GOPSALL FRESH FARMHOUSE ICE CREAM
Culloden Farm, Twycross, Leicestershire, CV9 3QJ.
01530 272 000
www.gopsallfresh.org.uk

Farmhouse ice cream, hand crafted on the Crown's Gopsall Estate in Leicestershire by the Thorp family. Made using the finest ingredients and the wholesome milk from their own herd of dairy cows.

LEICESTERSHIRE HANDMADE CHEESE CO

Sparkenhoe Farm, Main Road, Upton, Nuneaton,
Warwickshire, CV13 6JX.
01455 213 863
www.leicestershirecheese.co.uk

*Handmade from the milk produced by their own dairy
cows who graze the lush Leicestershire pastures near
Market Bosworth.*

LYMN BANK FARM CHEESE COMPANY

Lymn Bank Farm, Lymn Bank East, Thorpe St Peter,
Lincolnshire, PE24 4PJ.
01754 880 312
www.postacheese.com

*Family run company in rural Lincolnshire. Over the last
few years they have developed a unique product, with
a range of 19 flavoured handmade cheeses using the
best ingredients.*

THE MELTON CHEESEBOARD

8 Windsor Street, Melton Mowbray, Leicestershire, LE13 1BU.
01664 562 257
www.meltoncheeseboard.co.uk

*The Melton Cheeseboard stock the widest range of cheeses
in the county with over 120 different varieties, many of
them are sourced in Leicestershire and the surrounding
counties, as well as the best from the rest of the UK and a
wide variety of continental cheeses.*

MOUSETRAP CHEESE

Monkland Cheese Dairy, The Pleck, Monkland Leominster,
Herefordshire, HR6 9DB.
01568 720 307
www.mousetrapcheese.co.uk

*Throughout their three shops Mousetrap Cheese offer a
range of local, British farmhouse and continental cheeses,
mostly made from unpasteurised milk. A selection of these
cheeses are available to order online such as Hereford Sage
and Oak Smoked Little Hereford Sage.*

MR MOYDEN'S CHEESE

Martin and Beth Moyden
The Creamery, No. 3 Shropshire Food Enterprise Centre,
Vanguard Way, Battlefield Enterprise Park, Shrewsbury,
Shropshire, SY1 3TG.
01743 441 599
www.mrmoyden.com

*Mr. Moyden's handmade artisan cheeses are made using
traditional cheese making techniques which have been tried
and tested by countless generations of farmhouse and
specialist cheese makers.*

SHROPSHIRE CHEESE COMPANY

Abertanat Farm Dairy, Llanyblodwe, Oswestry,
Shropshire, SY10 8NA.
www.shropshirecheese.co.uk

*The Eyres family produce award-winning handmade
cheese, made using traditional processes and milk from
their own herd.*

DELICATESSEN - FINE AND SPECIALITY FOODS

CHERIZENA COFFEE BEANS

Cherizena Ltd, The Granary, The Wartnaby Estate,
Wartnaby, LE14 3HY.
01664 820 111
www.cherizena.co.uk

*At Cherizena you can buy single origin, unique blends and
speciality coffees and their range of flavoured Colombian
Arabica coffees is of the highest quality. All their coffees are
processed, blended, flavoured and packed at Wartnaby.
They use only the finest quality whole coffee beans
imported from growers around the world. Cherizena coffee
beans are committed to bringing you the finest quality
coffee for you to enjoy at home.*

COTTAGE DELIGHTS SPECIALITY FOODS

Leekbrook, Leek, Staffordshire, ST13 7QF.
01538 382 020
www.cottagedelight.co.uk

*Cottage Delights have been producing speciality foods
since 1974. Using only the finest ingredients and
traditional production methods to make a wide range of
award-winning jams, marmalades and chutneys.*

Will Holland, La Bécasse

DICKINSON AND MORRIS
Ye Olde Pork Pie Shoppe, 10 Nottingham Street,
Melton Mowbray, Leicestershire, LE13 1NW.
01664 482 068
www.porkpie.co.uk

*Dickinson and Morris has been baking pork pies at
Ye Olde Pork Pie Shoppe in Melton Mowbray since 1851.
They have the dual acclaim of being the oldest pork pie
bakery and the last remaining producer of the authentic
Melton Mowbray pork pie based in the town centre.*

FARRINGTON'S OILS LTD
Bottom Farm, Hargrave, Northamptonshire, NN9 6BP.
01933 622 809
www.farrington-oils.co.uk

*Producers of Mellow Yellow Cold Presses Rapeseed Oil.
Delicious, healthy and truly British - it contains Omega 3,
Vitamin E and has the lowest saturated fat content of any
commonly available cooking oil - making it the perfect
choice for a healthy diet.*

HEDGEROW PRODUCTS LTD
Blaby, Leicestershire, LE8 4BE.
www.hedgerow-products.co.uk

*Hedgerow Products is a young, exciting and innovative
Leicestershire company whose mission is to bring to you,
the customer, traditional good quality chutneys, jams and
jellies that look good, taste good and do not contain any
artificial additives, preservatives, sweeteners or colours.*

JUST OIL
Wade Lane Farm, Hill Ridware, Staffordshire, WS15 3RE.
01543 493 081
www.justoil.co.uk

*Just Oil is produced by the Froggatt family on their farm in
Hill Ridware in the heart of Staffordshire. This fine culinary
oil is grown, harvested, cold pressed, filtered and bottled on
their farm.*

THE LUDLOW NUT COMPANY
Unit 20, Rural Enterprise Centre, Eco Park Road, Ludlow,
Shropshire, SY8 1FF.
01584 876 512
www.ludlownutco.co.uk

*Based in Ludlow, the gastronomic capital of rural Britain,
The Ludlow Nut Company hand makes its own
award-winning range of luxury muesli, porridge mixes and
cereal bars and sells only the highest quality nuts, dried
fruits, seeds, nut/fruit and seed mixes, confectionery and a
reasonably priced range of superfoods including goji berries,
cacao nibs and barley and wheat grass powder.*

FARM SHOPS

ASTON MARINA FARM SHOP
Aston Marina, Lichfield Road, Stone,
Staffordshire, ST15 8QU.
01785 819 702
www.astonmarina.co.uk

*Delicatessen selling local British continental cheese as well
as mouth-watering cured and cooked meats, charcuterie,
patés and terrines, home-cooked quiches, pies and pastry
and beautifully prepared antipasto.*

BELVOIR FRUIT FARMS
Belvoir, Grantham, Lincolnshire, NG32 1PB.
01476 870 286
www.belvoirfruitfarms.co.uk

*At Belvoir Fruit Farm they make naturally delicious cordials,
pressés and fruit crushes at their home in the gorgeous
Lincolnshire countryside.*

BRYN DERW FARM
Llandinam, Powys, SY17 5AU.
01686 689 023
www.brynderwfarm.co.uk

*Free range eggs, Christmas turkey, pork and more are all
available from Bryn Derw Farm.*

DRAGON ORCHARD

Dragon House, Putley, Ledbury, Herefordshire, HR8 2RG.
01531 670 071
www.onceuponatree.co.uk

Dragon Orchard is a small, traditional fruit farm that has been tended by the Stanier family for over 80 years. They have been innovative in championing local food and over the past few years has helped bridge the gap between producers and consumers with the Cropsharers and Sponsor A Tree scheme.

ESSINGTON FRUIT FARM

Bognop Road, Essington, Wolverhampton, Staffordshire, WV11 2BA.
01902 735 724
www.essingtonfarm.co.uk

Family run farm since 1892. The farm is run on traditional principles and varieties are often old fashioned ones selected for flavour. Fruit and vegetables are available from their farm shop and you can pick your own soft fruit.

GREEN FIELDS FARM SHOP

Station Road, Donnington, Telford, Shropshire, TF2 8JY.
01952 677 345
Now also at Priorslee phone: 01952 200 696
www.greenfieldsonline.co.uk

Green Fields is more than a farm shop, it is the home of great local food for people in Shropshire, Staffordshire, Herefordshire and across the West Midlands.

PICKS ORGANIC

The Cottage, King Street, Hamilton Grounds, Barkby Thorpe, Leicestershire, LE7 3QF.
0116 269 3548
www.picksorganic.co.uk

Picks Organic are a family run farm and have been producing organic meat and vegetables since 1999. They strongly believe in the principles of organic farming. Their crops are grown and animals reared without the use of pesticides or fertilisers, growth hormones or routine antibiotics, in a way that enhances the environment, maintains the quality of the soil and does not harm wildlife.

RYTON ORGANIC GARDENS

Ryton on Dunsmore, Coventry, CV8 3LG.
01247 630 3517
www.rytongardens.co.uk

Ryton Gardens is set in the heart of England and combines ten acres of organic gardens buzzing with wildlife, brimming with plants, bursting with flowers and abundant in fruit and vegetables available to buy in their on-site shop.

STREFFORD HALL FARM SHOP

Craven Arms, Shropshire, SY7 8DE.
01588 672 759
www.streffordhallfarmshop.co.uk

Strefford Hall Farm Shop is a working farm located at the heart of an area of outstanding natural beauty in the footholds of the Shropshire hills. There are 146 hectares (350 acres) of cattle, sheep, finisher pigs, free range laying hens, geese and arable farming all nestling in the shelter of the Wenlock Edge. They offer farm fresh meat from traditionally farmed animals that have been dry hung to produce tasty, tender eating.

SUNNY SIDE UP

Poplar Farm, Tealby Road, Market Rasen, Lincolnshire, LN8 3UL.
01673 844 736
www.sunnyside-up.co.uk

Quality fresh meat, free range eggs, comestibles and ready meals located between Market Rasen and Tealby, on the edge of the Lincolnshire Wolds, providing you with locally sourced, quality products at a price you can afford.

WOODHOUSE FARM

Burbage Common Road, Elmesthorpe, Leicestershire, LE9 7SE.
01455 851 242
www.woodhousefarm.co.uk

Woodhouse Farm understand that excellent animal welfare is the best way to ensure fantastic flavour and tenderness. They therefore only use their own home bred meat so that they can be sure of supreme taste and succulence of their products.

George Watkins, Ballingham Farm

WOODLANDS ORGANIC FARM (KIRTON) LTD

Kirton House, Kirton, Boston, Lincolnshire, PE20 1JD.
01205 724 778
www.woodlandsfarm.co.uk

Woodlands Organic Farm produce organic vegetable boxes throughout Lincolnshire and the East Midlands (Rutland, Northamptonshire, Leicestershire, Cambridgeshire and Nottinghamshire) with vegetables, fruit, salads, flowers, beef, lamb, turkeys, poultry... each in their season. They grow, pick, pack and deliver their organic boxes to your door.

WYNNE'S OF DINMORE

Hope-under-Dinmore, Herefordshire, HR6 0PX.
01568 797 314
www.wynnes.co.uk

Producers of quality, free range eggs. Hens range freely on fields from morning until dusk and have access to water, shelter and a diet of quality (non GM) cereal based feed which is supplement from the pastures on which they roam. Available to purchase from their farm shop which opens Wednesday - Saturday, 9.00am - 4.30pm.

FISH

BIRMINGHAM FISH MARKET

Edgbaston Street, Birmingham, West Midlands, B5 4RB.

THE FISH HOUSE

Tolsey House, 51 Bullring, Ludlow. Shropshire, SY8 1AB.
01584 879 790, 07723 993 036
thefishhouseludlow@ymail.com

A high quality fishmongers and oyster bar in the heart of Ludlow's historic town centre.

WESTPORT FOODS

Units 1, 2 & 3 Dain Street, Burslem, Stoke-On-Trent, Staffordshire, ST6 3LN.
01782 834 032
sales@westportfoods.co.uk

MEAT

AUBREY ALLEN DIRECT

108 Warwick Street, Leamington, Warwickshire, CV32 4QP.
01926 311 208
www.aubreyallen.co.uk

Aubrey Allen have been serving the Warwickshire public the finest meat since 1933. They carefully select and inspect all of their suppliers and can trace their meat from farm to plate.

They are renowned for meat such as granite grassland reared Cornish lamb, corn fed Loire Valley hens, and free range pork produced by 'Pig Farmer of the Year' Jimmy Butler.

BROCKLEBYS

Asfordby Hill, Melton Mowbray, LE14 3QU.
01664 813 200
www.brocklebys.co.uk

Brocklebys farm, butcher and retail meat from both traditional and rare breed stock. All their animals are farmed using traditional methods of animal husbandry and their fields are free from artificial fertilisers, pesticides and GM crops. The meat they produce is slowly matured and both hormone and antibiotic free.

THE BARN BACON COMPANY

Old Hall Farm Shop, Old Hall Farm, Kneesall, Newark, Nottinghamshire, NG22 0AD.
01623 862 210
www.barnbacon.co.uk

The Barn Bacon Company is a family run business that prides itself on offering the very best in quality flavoursome meat.

BONS HIGH CLASS FAMILY BUTCHERS

Barber Street, Broseley, Shropshire, TF12 5NR.
01952 882 439
www.simongibbonsbutchers.co.uk

Simon Gibbons high class butchers in Broseley town, Shropshire, specialises in 'happy meats' with outdoor bred pork, wild game, and 21 day aged beef. Simon is keen to pass on his cooking skills to ensure that every customer benefits from the best selected cuts of meat for the best results in cooking and taste.

BOUVERIE LODGE

Nether Broughton, Melton Mowbray, Leicestershire, LE14 3EX.
01664 822 114
www.bisons.org

Bouverie Lodge Bison Farm is a working farm situated approximately five miles North West of Melton Mowbray, Leicestershire on the outskirts of the village of Nether Broughton. They sell farm delicious bison and venison meat from bison steaks and burgers to vension joints. All their meat is butchered and vacuum packed on-site.

CHECKETTS OF OMBERSLEY

Ombersley, Droitwich, Worcestershire, WR9 0EW.
01905 620 284
www.checketts.co.uk

The Checketts's have been around Worcestershire for more than 100 years. They sell locally sourced meats and many award-winning products such as home-made sausages, home cooked meats, home-made pies and excellent free range eggs.

D W WALL & SON
Wilton House, Craven Arms, Shropshire, SY7 9NL.
01588 672 308
www.wallsbutchers.co.uk

One of Shropshire's best rare breed butchers.

HAPPY MEATS
Bank House Farm, Stanford Bridge,
Worcestershire, WR6 6RU.
01886 812 485
www.happymeats.co.uk

Happy Meats is a specialist producer of superb free range, rare breed meat, where welfare is put first. Traditional old British and Irish breeds of pig, lamb and cattle are reared outside on chemical free food. The result is quality tasty meat which you can trust.

MAYNARDS FARM BACON LTD
Weston-Under-Redcastle, Shrewsbury, Shropshire, SY4 5LR.
01948 840 252
www.maynardsfarm.co.uk

Maynards Farm bacon and hams are still cured and smoked on the farm using many of the same methods and recipes used in the 17th Century when the Journeyman Master Curer travelled from farm to farm collecting recipes as he went.

ROBERT BOWRING FARMER AND BUTCHER
38, High Street, Mansfield Woodhouse, Mansfield,
Nottinghamshire, NG19 8AN.
01623 623 512
www.robertbowring.co.uk

TORI AND BEN'S FARM
Woodhouse Farm, Isley Cum Langley, Diseworth,
Derbyshire, DE74 2QQ.
07884 112 812
www.toriandbensfarm.co.uk

This young farming couple are passionate about livestock and delivering the highest quality produce to your door.

SMOKED FOODS

ALFRED ENDERBY LTD
Maclure Street, Fish Docks, Grimsby, Lincolnshire, DN31 3NE.
01472 342 984
www.alfredenderby.co.uk

Alfred Enderby Ltd in Grimsby is one of only a few independent family run traditional fish smoking firms left in England. The traditional smokehouse, with its distinctive tall chimneys, is about 100 years old with two generations of Enderby family involved in running it for two thirds of that time.

BELLEAU BRIDGE TROUT FARM
Belleau, Alford, Nr Louth, Lincolnshire LN13 0BP.
01507 480 225
www.belleausmokery.co.uk

Belleau Bridge Trout Farm was established in 1975 supplying live fish for restocking reservoirs, waterways and rivers for anglers. In the last two years Belleau Smokery was formed to run alongside the live fish business. The smokery is a dream come true for Simon Harrop, the third generation fish farmer and whilst it has been three years in the making it was only started in October 2008. Their aim is to produce the finest smoked food.

BINGS HEATH SMOKERY
Greenfields, Bings Heath, Astley, Shrewsbury, SY4 4BY.
01939 250 141
www.greenfieldsonline.co.uk

Alan and Shirley Ball specialise in the preparation of finest quality traditionally smoked foods.

All are guaranteed to be free from artificial colourings, flavourings and preservatives. The only curing agents used are natural sea salts and oak smoke. The smoking process is carried out in a traditional smoke house, typified of those used by small Scottish and Norwegian salmon curers. Also breeding their own Dexter beef.

THE ORGANIC SMOKEHOUSE
Clunbury Hall, Clunbury, Shropshire, SY7 0HG.
01588 660 206
www.organicsmokehouse.com

Award-winning smokehouse operating from the beautiful Welsh Marches.

VEGETABLES

THE ORGANIC BOX COMPANY
Wolseley Bridge Farm, Wolseley Bridge, Stafford,
Staffordshire, ST17 0XP.
07970 761 414
www.theorganicboxcompany.co.uk

The Organic Box Company is located in Staffordshire and are committed to supplying customers throughout Staffordshire with top quality organic fruit, vegetables, cheeses and groceries.

ROWLAND'S FRESH PRODUCE
Knights way, Battlefield Enterprise Park,
Shrewsbury, SY1 3AB.
01743 462 244
www.rowlandsltd.co.uk

CONTRIBUTORS

Alex Penhaligon, Aalto Restaurant At Hotel La Tour

Tom Court, The Granary

AALTO RESTAURANT AT HOTEL LA TOUR

Albert Street, Birmingham, B5 5JT
0121 718 8000
www.hotel-latour.co.uk

CASTLE HOUSE

Castle Street, Hereford, Herefordshire, HR1 2NW
01432 356 321
www.castlehse.co.uk

FAIRLAWNS

178 Little Aston Road, Aldridge, North Birmingham, WS9 0NU
01922 455 122
www.fairlawns.co.uk

THE FEATHERS HOTEL

The Bull Ring, Ludlow, Shropshire, SY8 1AA
01584 875 261
www.feathersatludlow.co.uk

FISHMORE HALL

Fishmore Road, Ludlow, Shropshire, SY8 3DP
01584 875 148
www.fishmorehall.co.uk

THE GRANARY

Heath Lane, Shenstone, Kidderminster, Worcestershire, DY10 4BS
01562 777 535
www.granary-hotel.co.uk

Will Holland, La Bécasse

Philip Olivant, The Lion At Brewood

THE HUNDRED HOUSE HOTEL, PUB & RESTAURANT

Bridgnorth Road, Norton, Shropshire, TF11 9EE
01952 580 240
www.hundredhouse.co.uk

THE KING AND THAI

Avenue Road, Broseley, Shropshire, TF12 5DL
01952 882 004
www.thekingandthai.co.uk

LA BÉCASSE

17 Corve Street, Ludlow, Shropshire, SY8 1DA
01584 872 325
www.labecasse.co.uk

LION AND PHEASANT

50 Wyle Cop, Shrewsbury, SY1 1XJ
01743 770 345
www.lionandpheasant.co.uk

THE LION AT BREWOOD

1 Market Place, Brewood, Staffordshire, ST19 9BS
01902 850 123
www.lionhotelbrewood.co.uk

THE LION BAR, RESTAURANT AND ROOMS

High Street, Leintwardine, Shropshire, SY7 0JZ
01547 540 203
www.thelionleintwardine.co.uk

Matt Davies, The Orangery Restaurant At The Moat House

Adam Gray, The Red Lion

NUTHURST GRANGE COUNTRY HOUSE HOTEL AND RESTAURANT
Nuthurst Lane, Hockley Heath, Warwickshire, B94 5NL
01564 783 972
www.nuthurst-grange.co.uk

THE ORANGERY RESTAURANT AT THE MOAT HOUSE
Lower Penkridge Road, Acton Trussell, Staffordshire, ST17 0RJ
01785 712 217
www.moathouse.co.uk

THE ORANGERY RESTAURANT AT LOSEHILL HOUSE HOTEL AND SPA
Losehill Lane, Edale Road, Hope, Peak District, Derbyshire, S33 6AF
01433 621 219
www.losehillhouse.co.uk

ORLES BARN
Wilton, Ross-on-Wye, Herefordshire, HR9 6AE
01989 562 155
www.orles-barn.co.uk

PEEL'S RESTAURANT BY MARTYN PEARN
Shadowbrook Lane, Hampton-in-Arden, Solihull, B92 0EN
01675 446 080
www.peelsrestaurant.co.uk

THE RED LION
Main Street, East Haddon, Northamptonshire, NN6 8BU
01604 770 223
www.redlioneasthaddon.co.uk

SEASONS RESTAURANT
Colwall Park, Colwall, Malvern, Worcestershire, WR13 6QG
01684 540 000
www.colwall.co.uk

Andreas Antona, Simpsons Restaurant With Rooms

Richard Turner, Turners

SIMPSONS RESTAURANT WITH ROOMS

20 Highfield Road, Edgbaston, Birmingham, B15 3DU
0121 454 3434
www.simpsonsrestaurant.co.uk

THE SWAN WITH TWO NECKS

Nantwich Road, Blackbrook, Staffordshire, ST5 5EH
01782 680 343
www.theswanwithtwonecks.co.uk

THE THREE HORSESHOES INN
AND COUNTRY HOTEL

Buxton Road, Blackshaw Moor, Leek, Staffordshire, ST13 8TW
01538 300 296
www.3shoesinn.co.uk

TURNERS

69 High Street, Harborne, Birmingham, B17 9NS
0121 426 4440
www.turnersrestaurantbirmingham.co.uk

THE WARWICK RESTAURANT BRASSERIE

Stratford Road, Hockley Heath, Warwickshire, B94 5NW
01564 785 252
www.warwickhockleyheath.co.uk

THE WAYFARER

The Wayfarer Stone, The Fillybrooks, Stone, Staffordshire, ST15 0NB
01785 811 023
www.thewayfarerstone.co.uk

RELISH PUBLICATIONS

Relish Publications is an independent publisher of exclusive regional recipe books, featuring only the best and brightest critically acclaimed chefs and the venues at which they work, all of which showcased with superb photography. They also work with some chefs individually to produce bespoke publications tailored to their individual specifications. Since 2009, Relish has fostered a national presence, while maintaining friendly, personalised service that their small but highly professional team prides themselves on.

Relish Wales

A region with its own rich, unique heritage and home to a vast and diverse landscape. From the rugged valleys and endless coastlines to the bustling streets of Cardiff and it's other big cities, Welsh cuisine represents a blend of cultures that is as interesting as it is delicious. Renowned chef Shaun Hill introduces this ambitious book that covers the wide range of talent that Wales has to offer.

Relish Cheshire and Greater Manchester

As one of the most populated areas in the UK, Greater Manchester has a wealth of talent to display. Traditionally seen as a historic centre of industry, Manchester's finer side inspires great chefs such as Andrew Nutter to produce truly amazing food. Alongside this, Cheshire offers a refreshing change of pace. Further away from the hustle and bustle, its own character is reflected in some equally stunning cuisine. This Relish book shows it all in this journey around the North West.

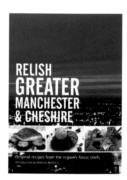

Relish Merseyside and Lancashire

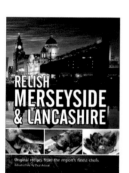

As one of the most historically significant ports in the country, Liverpool continues to have importance to this day, by giving us all access to a world of high quality food, but there is just as much talent further afield, as shown in the stunning chefs we have chosen to represent Lancashire. Renowned local chef, Paul Askew, starts of this book by introducing us to some of the quality produce that this region has to offer, and how he is so proud to be championing an area that has many great chefs and restaurants.

Relish Yorkshire Second Helping

The latest edition of Relish Yorkshire features a foreword by celebrity chef Tessa Bramley and returns to the county with all new recipes from Yorkshire's greatest chefs; Michelin Starred James McKenzie from The Pipe and Glass and Steve Smith from The Burlington, plus Richard Allen from The Fourth Floor at Harvey Nichols and many, many more. Relish Yorkshire Second Helping is a must have for any hearty food lover with true Yorkshire pride.

Relish Scotland

With over 300 pages of Scotland's finest recipes, this book takes you on an epic journey from Edinburgh to Glasgow, across to Aberdeen and then up to the Highlands and Islands, through rugged landscapes and beautiful cities. An introduction from TV celebrity chef Nick Nairn prepares the palate for recipes from nationally acclaimed restaurateurs such as Tom Kitchin, Martin Wishart and Geoffrey Smeddle. With breathtaking pictures of the views and venues, Relish Scotland promises to make for fascinating reading for both foodies and tourists alike.

Relish Cumbria

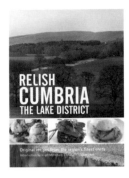

Over 50 mouth-watering exclusive recipes for you to try at home from some of Cumbria's finest country house hotels and acclaimed restaurants including The Samling, Russell Plowman at Gilpin Lodge Hotel and Andrew McGeorge at Rampsbeck Country House Hotel. Packed with innovative recipes and stunning photography to match the stunning landscape, Relish Cumbria is certain to make a fantastic addition to any cook's library.

Relish North East

From the bustling city life in Newcastle, to the multitude of sleepy, rural villages, the North East has something for everyone. An introduction from the North east's best known chef, Terry Laybourne, kicks off this culinary adventure through a rich and diverse region, with many varied recipes for you to try at home including a selection from the North East's two Masterchef finalists, John Calton and David Coulson, plus many others from award-winning chefs across the region.

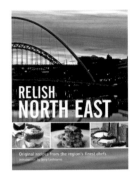

LOOKING TO DINE IN THE UK'S FINEST RESTAURANTS?

Simply log on to relishpublications.co.uk and find the very best your region has to offer.

The Relish team has worked with all of the restaurants and chefs listed on the Relish website and have visited every highly recommended and acclaimed restaurant. These ingredients make the **Relish Restaurant Guide** genuine and unique.

If you would like to be taken on an epic journey to the finest restaurants in each region, download more mouth-watering recipes, or add to your collection of Relish books, visit **www.relishpublications.co.uk**

gourmet-lifestyle.co.uk
degustation of food news, reviews, events & offers

Up to date Midlands restaurant news, reviews, profiles, and exclusive events and offers on the region's dedicated gourmands website www.gourmet-lifestyle.co.uk

Official supporter of Relish Midlands - original recipes from the region's finest chefs

ALGINATE BATH
A mix of sodium alginate and water that is used to make food retain a spherical shape while still being liquid in the middle.

BAIN-MARIE
A pan or other container of hot water with a bowl placed on top of it. This allows the steam from the water to heat the bowl and so ingredients can be gently heated or melted in the bowl.

BEURRE MONTE
Melted butter that remains emulsified even at temperatures higher than that at which butter usually breaks down.

BLANCH
Boiling an ingredient before removing it and plunging it in ice cold water in order to stop the cooking process.

CONFIT
A method of cooking where the meat is cooked submerged in a liquid to add flavour. Often this liquid is rendered fat.

COOKING LIQUOR
The liquid that is left over from cooking of meat or vegetables. Can be incorporated into sauces and gravy.

DARIOLE
A French term that refers to small, cylinder shaped moulds.

DEGLAZE
A fancy term for using the flavour-packed brown bits stuck to the bottom of a pan to make a pan sauce or gravy.

DEMI-GLACE OR GLACE
A thick, shiny deep brown French sauce used as a base for other sauces to give depth to complex dishes.

GRAVADLAX
A dish of raw salmon that has been cured in salt, sugar and dill. It is popular in Nordic and Scandinavian countries and is usually served as a starter.

JUS
The natural juices given off by the food. To prepare a natural jus, the cook may simply skim off the fat from the juices left after cooking and bring the remaining meat stock and water to a boil.

ORANGE COMPOUND
Orange compound has a fruity orange flavour for all your baking needs. The orange compound produces a distinct orange flavour in desserts, beverages and sauces.

Use pure orange compound to flavour marinades, compound butter, chutney, syrup and chocolate sauce.

PATE A BOMBE
French term for a mixture used as a base for making chocolate mousse and other mousse-like desserts.

REDUCTION
The process of thickening a liquid in order to intensify the flavour. This is done by evaporating the moisture in a liquid.

ROUX
A mix of flour and melted butter that is the base for many types of sauce.

SABAYON
A custard-like dessert from Italy. Made with egg, sugar, water and sometimes sweet wine.

SEAL
To cook meat at a high temperature for a short period of time, resulting in a cooked crust on the outside and raw meat on the inside.

SEMIFREDDO
Italian for 'half cold', meaning foods that are only partly frozen.

SILPAT
A brand of silicone mats.

TIMBALE
A type of pan or mould in which food is cooked, giving the food the same shape as the pan.

TUILLE
A wafer thin biscuit that can be made of a variety of things. Often served to decorate a dish.

VELOUTE
A type of sauce made from stock, roux and seasoning.